Katra House
December, 1992.

THE WIND FROM THE STARS

THE WIND FROM THE STARS

through the year
with

George MacDonald

edited by

GORDON REID

HarperCollins*Religious*
an imprint of HarperCollins*Publishers*

HarperCollins*Religious*
Part of HarperCollins*Publishers*
77–85 Fulham Palace Road, London w6 8jb

First published in Great Britain
in 1992 by HarperCollins*Religious*

1 3 5 7 9 10 8 6 4 2

ISBN
0 00 5993202 U.K. EDITION
0 00 5993474 ZONDERVAN EDITION
0 00 5993482 HARPER COLLINS SAN FRANCISCO EDITION

Designed and typeset in Stempel Garamond and Castellar by
Jeffrey Dean, The Stingray Office, Oxford

Printed and bound in Hong Kong

TO THE MEMORY OF
MY PARENTS

WILLIAM ALBERT REID
AND
ELIZABETH JEAN REID

I have tried to select passages that stand by themselves as good examples of the deep wisdom of George MacDonald. They are sometimes explicitly Christian, sometimes of wider application. But they can all be called examples of MacDonald's Christian teaching, because he abhorred any attempt to confine Christianity and to divorce it from everyday life and experience.

My title, 'The Wind from the Stars', comes from the end of *Robert Falconer* and is part of a great passage which sums up the faith, hope and boundless charity of MacDonald. Here it is in full:

> The evening began to grow dark. The autumn wind met us again, colder, stronger, yet more laden with the odours of death and the frosts of the coming winter. But it no longer blew as from the charnel-house of the past; it blew from the stars through the chinks of the unopened door on the other side of the sepulchre. It was a wind of the worlds, not a wind of the leaves. It told of the march of the spheres and the rest of the throne of God. We were going on into the universe — home to the house of our Father. Mighty adventure! Sacred repose! And as I followed the pair, one great star throbbed and radiated over my head.

There is George MacDonald, the poet, the mystic, the theologian, the lover of God, man and Nature. The following 366 passages, drawn from all his works, will give readers a year (and a day!) in the company of this remarkable man. I hope they will have as much profit and delight from him as I have had.

GORDON REID

PRAYER OF THE CHILDREN

'We thank thee that we have a father and not a maker, that thou hast begotten us, and not moulded us as images of clay; that we have come forth of thy heart, and have not been fashioned by thy hands. It must be so. Only the heart of a father is able to create. We rejoice in it, and bless thee that we know it. We thank thee for thyself. Be what thou art — our root and life, our beginning and end, our all in all. Come home to us. Thou livest; therefore we live. In thy light we see. Thou art — that is all our song.'

Thus they worship, and love, and wait. Their hope and expectation grow ever stronger and brighter, that one day, ere long, the Father will show himself amongst them, and thenceforth dwell in his own house for evermore. What was once but an old legend has become the one desire of their hearts.

And the loftiest hope is the surest of being fulfilled.

Adela Cathcart

2
THE IDEAL FATHER

God be praised by those who know religion to be the truth of humanity — its own truth that sets it free — not binds, and lops, and mutilates it! who see God to be the father of every human soul — the ideal Father, not an inventor of schemes, or the upholder of a court etiquette for whose use he has chosen to desecrate the name of *justice*.

Robert Falconer

3
NO LONELY GOD

Never man and woman yet succeeded in being all in all to each other.

It were presumption to say that a lonely God would be enough for himself, seeing that we can know nothing of God but as he is our Father. What if the creator himself is sufficient to himself in virtue of his self-existent *creatorship*? Let my reader think it out. The lower we go in the scale of creation, the more independent is the individual. The richer and more perfect each of a married pair is in the other relations of life, the more is each to the other.

Paul Faber, Surgeon

Then came the reflection, how little at any time could a father do for the well-being of his children! The fact of their being children implied their need of an all-powerful father: must there not then be such a father? Therewith the truth dawned upon him, that first of truths, which all his church-going and Bible-reading had hitherto failed to disclose, that, for life to be a good thing and worth living, a man must be the child of a perfect father, and know him. In his terrible perturbation about his children, he lifted up his heart — not to the Governor of the world; not to the God of Abraham or Moses; not in the least to the God of the Kirk; least of all to the God of the Shorter Catechism; but to the faithful creator and father of David Barclay. The aching soul which none but a perfect father could have created capable of deploring its own fatherly imperfection, cried out to the father of fathers on behalf of his children, and as he cried, a peace came stealing over him such as he had never before felt.

Heather and Snow

NO NOTHINGNESS

I repent me of the ignorance wherein I ever said that God made men out of nothing: there is no nothing out of which to make anything; God is all in all, and he made us out of himself. He who is parted from God has no original nothingness with which to take refuge.

Weighed and Wanting

THE FIRE OF GOD

The fire of God which is his essential being, his love, his creative power, is a fire unlike its earthly symbol in this, that it is only at a distance it burns — that the further from him, it burns the worse, and that when we turn and begin to approach him, the burning begins to change to comfort, which comfort will grow to such bliss that the heart cries out with a gladness no other gladness can reach, 'Whom have I in heaven but thee? and there is none upon earth that I desire besides thee!'

Unspoken Sermons

When we come to consider the acts embodying the Divine thought (if indeed thought and act be not with him one and the same), then we enter a region of large difference. We discover at once, for instance, that where a man would make a machine, or a picture, or a book, God makes the man that makes the book, or the picture or the machine. Would God give us a drama? He makes a Shakespeare. Or would he construct a drama more immediately his own? He makes the actors, and they do not act — they *are* their part. He utters them into the visible to work out their life — his drama. When he would have an epic, he sends a thinking hero into his drama, and the epic is the soliloquy of his Hamlet. Instead of writing his lyrics, he sets his birds and his maidens a-singing. All the processes of the ages are God's science; all the flow of history is his poetry. His sculpture is not in marble, but in living and speech-giving forms, which pass away, not to yield place to those that come after, but to be perfected in a nobler studio. What he has done remains, although it vanishes; and he never either forgets what he has once done, or does it even once again. As the thoughts move in the mind of a man, so move the worlds of men and women in the mind of God, and make no confusion there, for there they had their birth, the offspring of his imagination. Man is but a thought of God.

A Dish of Orts

For, when we say that God is Love, do we teach men that their fear of him is groundless? No. As much as they fear will come upon them, possibly far more. But there is something beyond their fear which they cannot withstand, because it works along with the human individuality which the divine individuality has created in them. The wrath will consume what they *call* themselves; so that the selves God made shall appear, coming out with ten-fold consciousness of being, and bringing with them all that made the blessedness of the life the men tried to lead without God. They will know that now first are they fully themselves. The avaricious, weary, selfish, suspicious old man shall have passed away. The young, ever young self, will remain. That which they *thought* themselves shall have vanished: that which they *felt* themselves, though they misjudged their own feelings, shall remain — remain glorified in repentant hope. For that which cannot be shaken shall remain. That which is immortal in God shall remain in man. The death that is in them shall be consumed.

Unspoken Sermons

FATHER AND SON

A God must have a God for company.
And lo! thou hast the Son-God to thy friend.
Thou honour'st his obedience, he thy law.
Into thy secret life-will he doth see;
Thou fold'st him round in live love perfectly —
One two, without beginning, without end:
In love, life, strength, truth, each is perfect without
    a flaw.

Diary of An Old Soul

10
INFINITE GIVING

I saw, shadowed out in the absolute devotion of Jesus
to men, that the very life of God by which we live is
an everlasting giving of himself away. He asserts himself, only, solely, altogether, in an infinite sacrifice of
devotion. So must we live; the child must be as the
father; live he cannot on any other plan, struggle as he
may. The father requires of him nothing that he is not
or does not himself, who is the one prime uncondi-
tioned sacrificer and sacrifice.

Wilfred Cumbermede

11
APPROACHES

When thou turn'st away from ill,
Christ is this side of thy hill.
When thou turnest towards good,
Christ is walking in thy wood.
When thy heart says, 'Father, pardon!'
Then the Lord is in thy garden.
When stern Duty wakes to watch,
Then His hand is on the latch.
But when Hope thy song doth rouse,
Then the Lord is in the house.
When to love is all thy wit,
Christ doth at thy table sit.
When God's will is thy heart's pole,
Then is Christ thy very soul.

Poetical Works

12
HEART OF HEARTS

'Thou art such a Father, that thou takest our sins from us and throwest them behind thy back. Thou cleanest our souls, as thy Son did wash our feet. We hold our hearts up to thee! Make them what they must be, O Love, O Life of men, O Heart of hearts!'

Malcolm

The name is one 'which no man knoweth saving he
that receiveth it'. Not only then has each man his
individual relation to God, but each man has his peculiar relation to God. He is to God a peculiar being,
made after his own fashion, and that of no one else;
for when he is perfected he shall receive the new name
which no one else can understand. Hence he can worship God as no one else can worship him — can understand God as no man else can understand him.

Unspoken Sermons

'Father, forgive them, for they know not what they
do,' said the Divine, making excuses for his murderers, not after it was all over, but at the very moment
when he was dying by their hands. Then Jesus had
forgiven them already. His prayer the Father must
have heard, for he and the Son are one. When the
Father succeeded in answering his prayer, then his
forgiveness in the hearts of the murderers broke out
in sorrow, repentance, and faith. Here was a sin
dreadful enough surely — but easy for our Lord to
forgive. All that excuse for the misled populace! Lord
Christ be thanked for that! That was like thee!

Unspoken Sermons

THE WAY

Back still it comes to this: there was a man
Who said, 'I am the truth, the life, the way':
Shall I pass on, or shall I stop and hear? —
'Come to the Father but by me none can':
What then is this? — am I not also one
Of those who live in fatherless dismay?
I stand, I look, I listen, I draw near.

Diary of an Old Soul

GOD SUFFERS

Malcolm said: 'Everybody knows what few think about, that once there lived a man who, in the broad face of prejudiced respectability, truth-hating hypocrisy, common-place religion, and dull book-learning, affirmed that he knew the secret of life, and understood the heart and history of men — who wept over their sorrows, yet worshipped the God of the whole earth, saying that he had known him from eternal days. The same said that he came to do what the Father did, and that he did nothing but what he had learned of the Father. They killed him, you know, my lady, in a terrible way that one is afraid even to think of. But he insisted that he laid down his life; that he allowed them to take it. Now I ask whether that grandest thing, crowning his life, the yielding of it to the hand of violence, he has not learned also from his Father. Was his death the only thing he had not so learned? If I am right, and I do not say 'if' in doubt, then the sufferings of those three terrible hours was a type of the suffering of the Father himself in bringing sons and daughters through the cleansing and the glorifying fires, without which the created cannot be made the very children of God, partakers of the divine nature and peace. Then from the lowest, weakest tone of suffering, up to the loftiest pitch, the divinest acme of pain, there is not one pang to which the sensorium of the universe does not respond; never an untuneful vibration of nerve or spirit but thrills beyond the brain or the heart of the sufferer to the brain, the heart of the universe; and God, in the simplest, most literal, fullest sense, and not by sympathy alone, suffers *with* his creatures.

The Marquis of Lossie

17
UNION OF FATHER AND SON

In very truth there must appear schism in Nature, yea schism in God himself, until we see that the ruling Father and the suffering Son are of one mind, one love, one purpose; that in the Father the Son rules, in the Son the Father suffers; that with the Son the other children must suffer and rise to rule.

There and Back

'O thou wha keeps the stars alicht, an' oor souls burnin' wi' a licht aboon that o' the stars, grant that they may shine afore thee as the stars for ever and ever. An' as thou hauds the stars burnin' a' the nicht whan there's no man to see, so haud thou the licht burnin' in our souls, whan we see neither thee nor it, but are buried in the grave o' sleep an' forgetfu'ness. Be thou by us, even as a mother sits by the bedside o' her ailin' wean a' the lang nicht; only be thou nearer to us, even in our verra souls, an' watch ower the warl' o' dreams that they mak for themsels. Grant that more an' more thochts o' thy thinkin' may come into our herts day by day, till there shall be at last an open road atween thee an' us, an' thy angels may ascend and descend upon us, so that we may be in thy heaven, e'en while we are upo' thy earth: Amen.'

David Elginbrod

'O thou in whase sicht oor deith is precious, an' no licht maiter; wha through darkness leads to licht, an' through deith to the greater life! — we canna believe that thou wouldst gie us ony thing, to tak' the same again; for that would be but bairns' play. We believe that thou taks, that thou may gie again the same thing better nor afore — mair o't and better nor we could ha' received it itherwise; just as the Lord took himsel' frae the sicht o' them 'at lo'ed him weel, that instead o' bein' veesible afore their een, he micht hide himsel' in their verra herts. Come thou, an' abide in us, an' tak' us to bide in thee; an' syne gin we be a' in thee, we canna be that far frae ane anither, though some sud be in haven, an' some upo' earth. Lord help us to do oor wark like thy men an' maidens doon the stair, remin'in' oursel's, 'at them 'at we miss has only gane up the stair, as gin 'twar to haud things to thy han' i' thy ain presence-chaumer, where we houp to be called or lang, an' to see thee an' thy Son, wham we lo'e aboon a'; an' in his name we say, Amen!'

David Elginbrod

Was the perfect son, for being perfect, he must be perfect in every way, to be the only son of man who needed to do nothing to please his mother — nothing but what fell in with his plan for the hour? Not so could he be the root, the living heart of the great response of the children to the Father of all! not so could the idea of the grand family ever be made a reality! Alas for the son who would not willingly for his mother do something which in itself he would rather not do! If it would have hurt his mother, if it had been in any way turning from the will of his Father in heaven, he would not have done it: that would have been to have answered her prayer against her. His yielding makes the story doubly precious to my heart. The Son then could change his intent, and spoil nothing: so, I say, can the Father: for the Son does nothing but what he sees the Father do.

The Miracles of Our Lord

HEART-POWER

'Tis heart on heart thou rulest. Thou art the same
At God's right hand as here exposed to shame,
And therefore workest now as thou didst then —
Feeding the faint divine in humble men.
Through all thy realms from thee goes out heart-
    power,
Working the holy, satisfying hour
When all shall love, and all be loved again.

Diary of an Old Soul

HEALING

[Falconer] always insisted that the Saviour healed
only those on whom his humanity had laid hold; that
he demanded faith of them in order to make them
regard him, that so his personal being might enter
into their hearts. Healing without faith in its source
would have done them harm instead of good — would
have been to them a windfall, not a Godsend; at best
the gift of magic, even sometimes the power of Satan
casting out Satan.

Robert Falconer

PRUDENCE

He had not yet begun to think about prudence, and perhaps, if some of us thought more about right, we should have less occasion to cultivate the inferior virtue. Perhaps also we should have more belief that there is One to care that things do not go wrong.

Sir Gibbie

THE GIVER IN THE GIFT

For the real good of every gift it is essential, first, that the giver be in the gift — as God always is, for he is love — and next, that the receiver know and receive the giver in the gift. Every gift of God is but a harbinger of his greatest and only sacrificing gift — that of himself. No gift unrecognized as coming from God is at its own best; therefore many things that God would gladly give us, things even that we need because we are, must wait until we ask for them, that we may know whence they come. When in all gifts we find him, then in him we shall find all things.

Unspoken Sermons

UNCONSCIOUS HOPE

There is so much passes in us of which our consciousness takes no grasp . . . that I feel encouraged to doubt whether there ever was a man absolutely without hope. That there have been, alas, are many, who are aware of no ground of hope, nay even who feel no glimmer in them of anything they can call hope, I know; but I think in them all is an underlying unconscious hope. I think that not one in all the world has more than a shadowy notion of what hopelessness means. Perhaps utter hopelessness is the outer darkness.

Thomas Wingfold, Curate

Faith is that by which a man lives inwardly, and orders his way outwardly. Faith is the root, belief the tree, and opinion the foliage that falls and is renewed with the seasons. Opinion is, at best, even the opinion of a true man, but the cloak of his belief, which he may indeed cast to his neighbour, but not with the truth inside it: that remains in his own bosom, the oneness between him and his God. St Paul knows well — who better? — that by no argument, the best that logic itself can afford, can a man be set right with the truth; that the spiritual perception which comes of hungering contact with the living truth — a perception which is in itself a being born again — can alone be the mediator between a man and the truth. He knows that, even if he could pass his opinion over bodily into the understanding of his neighbour, there would be little or nothing gained thereby, for the man's spiritual condition would be just what it was before. God must reveal, or nothing is known.

A Dish of Orts

I believe that no man is ever condemned for any sin except one — that he will not leave his sins and come out of them, and be the child of him who is his father.

I believe that justice and mercy are simply one and the same thing; without justice to the full there can be no mercy, and without mercy to the full there can be no justice.

Unspoken Sermons

People talk about special providences. I believe in the providences, but not in the specialty. I do not believe that God lets the thread of my affairs go for six days, and on the seventh evening takes it up for a moment. The so-called special providences are no exception to the rule — they are common to all men at all moments. But it is a fact that God's care is more evident in some instances of it than in others to the dim and often bewildered vision of humanity. Upon such instances men seize and call them providences. It is well that they can; but it would be gloriously better if they could believe that the whole matter is one grand providence.

Annals of a Quiet Neighbourhood

By his creation, each man is isolated with God; each, in respect of his peculiar making, can say, '*my* God'; each can come to him alone, and speak with him face to face, as a man speaketh with his friend. There is no *massing* of men with God. When he speaks of gathered men, it is as a spiritual *body*, not a *mass*. For in a body every smallest portion is individual, and therefore capable of forming a part of the body.

Unspoken Sermons

30
THOUGHT-EGGS

One great help to the understanding of things is to brood over them as a hen broods over her eggs: words are thought-eggs, and their chickens are truths: and in order to brood, I sometimes learn by heart.

Donal Grant

Am I going to sleep? — to lose consciousness — to be helpless for a time — thoughtless — dead? Or, more awful consideration, in the dreams that may come may I not be weak of will and scant of conscience? — Father, into thy hands I commend my spirit. I give myself back to thee. Take me, soothe me, refresh me, 'make me over again.' Am I going out into the business and turmoil of the day, where so many temptations may come to do less honourably, less faithfully, less kindly, less diligently than the Ideal Man would have me do? — Father, into thy hands. Am I going to do a good deed? Then of all times — Father, into thy hands; lest the enemy should have me now. Am I going to do a hard duty, from which I would gladly be turned aside — to refuse a friend's request, to urge a neighbour's conscience? — Father, into thy hands I commend my spirit. Am I in pain? Is illness coming upon me to shut out the glad visions of a healthy brain, and bring me such as are troubled and untrue? — Take my spirit, Lord, and see, as thou are wont, that it has no more to bear than it can bear.

Unspoken Sermons

[The curate of St Gregory's] seems ambitious of killing himself with work — of wearing himself out in the service of his master — and as quickly as possible. A good deal of that kind of thing is a mere holding of the axe to the grindstone, not a lifting of it up against thick trees. Only he won't be convinced till it comes to the helve. I met him the other day; he was looking as white as his surplice. I took upon me to read him a lecture on the holiness of holidays. 'I can't leave my poor,' he said. 'Do you think God can't do without you?' I asked. 'Is he so weak that he cannot spare the help of a weary man? But I think he must prefer quality to quantity, and for healthy work you must be healthy yourself. How can you be the visible sign of the Christ-present amongst men, if you inhabit an exhausted, irritable brain? Go to God's infirmary and rest awhile. Bring back health from the country to those that cannot go to it. If on the way it be transmuted into spiritual forms, so much the better. A little more of God will make up for a good deal less of you.'

Robert Falconer

FAR BEN

Strangely mingled — mingled even to confusion with faith in God, was his absolute trust in his wife — a confidence not very different in kind from the faith which so many Christians place in the mother of our Lord. To Robert, Janet was one who knew — one who was *far ben* with the Father of lights.

Sir Gibbie

34
THY WILL BE DONE

Thy will be done. I yield up everything.
'The life is more than meat' — then more than
   health;
'The body more than raiment' — then than wealth;
The hairs I made not, thou art numbering.
Thou art my life — I the brook, thou the spring.
Because thine eyes are open, I can see;
Because thou art thyself, 'tis therefore I am me.

Diary of an Old Soul

FROM FRIENDSHIP TO GOD

Then Falconer began to see that he must cultivate relations with other people in order to enlarge his means of helping the poor. He nowise abandoned his conviction that whatever good he sought to do or lent himself to aid must be effected entirely by individual influence. He had little faith in societies, regarding them chiefly as a wretched substitute, just better than nothing, for that help which the neighbour is to give to his neighbour. Finding how the unbelief of the best of the poor is occasioned by hopelessness in privation, and the sufferings of those dear to them, he was confident that only the personal communion of friendship could make it possible for them to believe in God. Christians must be in the world as He was in the world; and in proportion as the truth radiated from them, the world would be able to believe in him. Money he saw to be worse than useless, except as a gracious outcome of human feelings and brotherly love . . . But he must not therefore act as if he were the only person who could render this individual aid, or as if men influencing the poor individually could not aid each other in their individual labours. He soon found, I say, that there were things he could not do without help.

Robert Falconer

Mr Walton said, 'There is just the same kind of beauty in a good old face that there is in an old church. You can't say the church is so trim and neat as it was in the day that the first blast of the organ filled it with a living soul. The carving is not quite so sharp, the timbers are not quite so clean. There is a good deal of mould and worm-eating and cobwebs about the old place. Yet both you and I think it more beautiful now than it was then. Well, I believe it is, as nearly as possible, the same with an old face. It has got stained, and weatherbeaten, and worn; but if the organ of truth has been playing on inside the temple of the Lord, which St Paul says our bodies are, there is in the old face, though both form and complexion are gone, just the beauty of the music inside. The wrinkles and the brownness can't spoil it. A light shines through it all — that of the indwelling spirit. I wish we all grew old like the old churches.'

The Seaboard Parish

COINCIDENCES

How many things which, at the first moment, strike us as curious coincidences, afterwards become so operative in our lives, and so interwoven with the whole web of their histories, that instead of appearing any more as strange accidents, they assume the shape of unavoidable necessities, of homely, ordinary lawful occurrences, as much in their own place as any shaft or pinion of a great machine.

David Elginbrod

MITIGATION

We do our brother, our sister, grievous wrong, every time that, in our selfish justice, we forget the excuse that mitigates the blame. That God never does, for it would be to disregard the truth. As he will never admit a false excuse, so will he never neglect a true one. It may be he makes excuses which the sinner dare not think of; while the most specious of false ones shrivel into ashes before him. A man is bound to think of all just excuse for his offender, for less than the righteousness of God will not serve his turn.

Paul Faber, Surgeon

If I might guess, then guess I would
That, mid the gathered folk,
This gentle Dorcas one day stood,
And heard when Jesus spoke.

She saw the woven seamless coat —
Half envious, for his sake:
'Oh happy hands,' she said, 'that wrought
The honoured thing to make!'

Her eyes with longing tears grow dim:
She never can come nigh
To work one service poor for him
For whom she glad would die!

But hark, he speaks! Oh precious word!
And she has heard indeed!
'When did we see thee naked, Lord,
And clothed thee in thy need?'

The king shall answer, 'Inasmuch
As to my brethren ye
Did it — even to the least of such —
Ye did it unto me.'

Home, home she went, and plied the loom,
And Jesus' poor arrayed.
She died — they wept about the room,
And showed the coats she made.

Poetical Works

THE DOUBTER CAN HELP

An ordinary man that has had doubts, and has encountered and overcome them, or verified and found them the porters of the gates of truth, may be profoundly useful to any mind similarly assailed: but no knowledge of books, no degree of acquaintance with the wisest conclusions of others, can enable a man who has not encountered scepticism in his own mind, to afford any essential help to those caught in the net.

Paul Faber, Surgeon

TOO PERFECT

If I knew of a theory in which was never an uncompleted arch or turret, in whose circling wall was never a ragged breach, that theory I should know but to avoid: such gaps are the eternal windows through which the dawn shall look in.

Malcolm

KINGSHIP

With *thee on board, each sailor is a king,*
Nor I mere captain of my vessel then,
But heir of earth and heaven, eternal child;
Daring all truth, nor fearing anything;
Mighty in love, the servant of all men;
Resenting nothing, taking rage and blare
Into the Godlike silence of a loving care.

Diary of an Old Soul

43
USELESS ARGUMENT

Even genuine argument for the truth is not preaching
the gospel, neither is he whose unbelief is thus assailed, likely to be brought thereby into any mood
but one unfit for receiving it. Argument should be
kept to books; preachers ought to have nothing to do
with it — at all events in the pulpit. There let them
hold forth light, and let him who will, receive it, and
him who will not, forbear. God alone can convince,
and till the full time is come for the birth of the truth
in a soul, the words of even the Lord himself are not
there potent.

Paul Faber, Surgeon

It required but a brief examination of Donal to satisfy Mr Sclater that he was more than prepared for the university. But I fear me greatly the time is at hand when such as Donal will no more be able to enter her courts. Unwise and unpatriotic are any who would rather have a few prime scholars sitting about the wells of learning, than see those fountains flow freely for the poor, who are yet the strength of a country. It is better to have many upon the high road of learning, than a few even at its goal, if that were possible.

Sir Gibbie

45
INSTANT HELP

Some men are so pitiful over their poor neighbour that, finding they cannot lift him beyond the reach of the providence which intends they shall have the poor with them always, they will do for him nothing at all: 'Where is the use?' they say ... While the rich giver is saying, 'Poor fellow, he will be just as bad next month again or sooner!' the poor fellow is breathing the air of paradise, reaping more joy of life in half a day than his benefactor in half a year. Help in such soil is a quick seed and of rapid growth, burgeoning in a moment into the infinite aeons. Everything in this world is but temporary: why should temporary help be undervalued? Would you leave a drowning bather to drown because he would be sure to bathe again to-morrow? Is help help or is it not? If it be help then it is divine, and comes of God our saviour.

Castle Warlock

THE KINDNESS OF THE POOR

The best thing [about the poor] is their kindness to each other. There is an absolute divinity in their self-denial for those who are poorer than themselves. I know one man and woman, married people, who pawned their very furniture and wearing apparel to procure cod-liver oil for a girl dying in consumption. She was not even a relative, only an acquaintance of former years. They had found her destitute and taken her to their own poor home. There are fathers and mothers who will work hard all the morning and when dinner-time comes 'don't want any', that there may be enough for their children — or half enough, more likely. Children will take the bread out of their own mouths to put in that of their sick brother, or to stick in the fist of baby crying for a crust — giving only a queer little helpless grin, half of hungry sympathy, half of pleasure, as they see it disappear. The marvel to me is that the children turn out so well as they do; but that applies to the children in all ranks of life.

Robert Falconer

SLEEP

The cessation of labour affords but the necessary condition; makes it possible, as it were, for the occupant of an outlying station in the wilderness to return to his father's house for fresh supplies of all that is needful for life and energy. The child-soul goes home at night and returns in the morning to the labours of the school.

William Cumbermede

48
SHOWING THE GOOD

The loudest demand of the present day is for the representation of that grade of humanity of which men see the most — the type of things which could never have been but that it might pass. The demand marks the commonness, narrowness, low-levelled satisfaction of the age. It loves its own — not that which might be, and ought to be its own — not its better self, infinitely higher than its present, for the sake of whose approach it exists. I do not think that the age is worse in this respect than those which have preceded it, but that vulgarity, and a certain vile contentment swelling to self-admiration, have become more vocal than hitherto; just as unbelief, which I think in reality less prevailing than in former ages, has become largely more articulate, and thereby more loud and peremptory. But whatever the demand of the age, I insist that that which *ought* to be presented to its beholding, is the common good uncommonly developed, and that not because of its rarity, but because it is truer to humanity.

Sir Gibbie

49
TRUE COMFORT

I think I see old Eppie now, filling her sack with what the wind blew her; not with the grain: Eppie did not covet that; she only wanted her bed filled with the fresh springy chaff, on which she would sleep as sound as her rheumatism would let her, and as warm and dry and comfortable as any duchess in the land that happened to have the rheumatism too. For comfort is inside more than outside; and eider-down, delicious as it is, has less to do with it than some people fancy. How I wish all the poor people in the great cities could have good chaff beds to lie upon!

Ranald Bannerman's Boyhood

No one can deny the power of the wearied body to paralyze the soul; but I have a correlate theory which I love, and which I expect to find true — that, while the body wearies the mind, it is the mind that restores vigour to the body, and then, like the man who has built him a stately palace, rejoices to dwell in it. I believe that, if there be a living, conscious love at the heart of the universe, the mind, in the quiescence of its consciousness in sleep, comes into a less disturbed contact with its origin, the heart of the creation; whence gifted with calmness and strength for itself, it grows able to impart comfort and restoration to the weary frame.

Wilfred Cumbermede

There are various kinds and degrees of wrong-doing, which need varying kinds and degrees of forgiveness. An outburst of anger in a child, for instance, scarcely wants forgiveness. The wrong in it may be so small that the parent has only to influence the child for self-restraint, and the rousing of the will against the wrong. The father will not feel that such a fault has built up any wall between him and his child.

But suppose that he discovered in him a habit of sly cruelty towards his younger brothers, or the animals of the house, how differently would he feel! Could his forgiveness be the same as in the former case? Would not the different evil require a different *form* of forgiveness? I mean, would not the forgiveness have to take the form of that kind of punishment fittest for restraining, in the hope of finally rooting out, the wickedness? Could there be true love in any other kind of forgiveness than this? A passing-by of the offence might spring from a poor human kindness, but never from divine love. It would not be *remission*. Forgiveness can never be indifference. Forgiveness is love towards the unlovely.

Unspoken Sermons

The end of imagination is *harmony*. A right imagination, being the reflex of the creation, will fall in with the divine order of things as the highest form of its own operation; 'will tune its instrument here at the door' to the divine harmonies within; will be content alone with growth towards the divine idea, which includes all that is beautiful in the imperfect imaginations of men; will know that every deviation from that growth is downward; and will therefore send the man forth from its loftiest representations to do the commonest duty of the most wearisome calling in a hearty and hopeful spirit. This is the work of the right imagination; and towards this work every imagination, in proportion to the rightness that is in it, will tend. The reveries even of the wise man will make him stronger for his work; his dreaming as well as his thinking will render him sorry for past failure, and hopeful of future success.

A Dish of Orts

GOD OF NATURE

All about us, in earth and air, wherever the eye or ear can reach, there is a power ever breathing itself forth in signs, now in daisy, now in a wind-waft, a cloud, a sunset; a power that holds constant and sweetest relation with the dark and silent world within us. The same God who is in us, and upon whose tree we are the buds, if not yet the flowers, also is all about us — inside the Spirit; outside the Word. And the two are ever trying to meet in us; and when they meet, then the signs without, and the longing within, become one in light, and the man no more walketh in darkness, but knoweth whither he goeth.

Thomas Wingfold, Curate

REVELATION IN NATURE

I believe that every fact in Nature is a revelation of God, is there such as it is because God is such as he is; and I suspect that all its facts impress us so that we learn God unconsciously. True, we cannot think of any one fact thus, except as we find the soul of it — its fact of God; but from the moment when first we came into contact with the world, it is to us a revelation of God, his things seen, by which we come to know the things unseen.

Unspoken Sermons

The water itself, that dances and sings, and slakes the wonderful thirst — symbol and picture of that draught for which the woman of Samaria made her prayer to Jesus — this lovely thing itself, whose very wetness is a delight to every inch of the human body in its embrace — this live thing which, if I might, I would have running through my room, yea, babbling along my table — this water is its own self its own truth, and is therein a truth of God. Let him who would know the love of the maker, become sorely athirst, and drink of the brook by the way — then lift up his head — not at that moment to the maker of oxygen and hydrogen, but to the inventor and mediator of thirst and water, that man might foresee a little of what his soul may find in God.

Unspoken Sermons

56
THE MOON AND THE SUN

'I'll tell ye, Tibbie, what the mune aye minds me o'! The face o' God's like the sun, as ye hae tell't me; for no man cud see him an' live.'

'That's no sayin', ye ken,' interposed Tibbie, 'that we canna see him efter we're deid.'

'But the mune,' continued Annie, disregarding Tibbie's interruption, 'maun be like the face o' Christ, for it gies licht and ye can luik at it notwithstandin'. The mune's just like the sun wi' the ower-muckle taen oot o' 't.'

Alec Forbes of Howglen

57
GOD'S AIR

The fishes breathe but where thy waters roll;
The birds fly but within thy airy sea;
My soul breathes only in thy infinite soul;
I breathe, I think, I love, I live but thee.
Oh breathe, oh think — O Love, live into me;
Unworthy is my life till all divine,
Till thou see in me only what is thine.

Diary of an Old Soul

They who believe in the influence of the stars over the fates of men, are, in feeling at least, nearer the truth than they who regard the heavenly bodies as related to them merely by a common obedience to an external law. All that man sees has to do with man. Worlds cannot be without an intermundane relationship. The community of the centre of all creation suggests an interradiating connection and dependence of the parts. Else a grander idea is conceivable than that which is already imbodied. The blank, which is only a forgotten life, lying behind the consciousness, and the misty splendour, which is an undeveloped life, lying before it, may be full of mysterious revelations of other connections with the worlds around us, than those of science and poetry. No shining belt or gleaming moon, no red and green glory in a self-encircling twin star, but has a relation with the hidden things of a man's soul, and, it may be, with the secret history of his body as well. They are portions of the living house wherein he abides.

Phantastes

MORAL LAWS

In the moral world . . . a man may clothe in new forms, and for this employ his imagination freely, but he must invent nothing. He may not, for any purpose, turn its laws upside down. He must not meddle with the relations of live souls. The laws of the spirit of man must hold, alike in this world and in any world he may invent. It were no offence to suppose a world in which everything repelled instead of attracting the things around it; it would be wicked to write a tale representing a man it called good as always doing bad things, or a man it called bad as always doing good things: the notion itself is absolutely lawless. In physical things, a man may invent; in moral things he must obey — and take their laws with him into his invented world as well.

A Dish of Orts

DAISIES

The daisies were all asleep, spotting the green grass with stars of carmine; for their closed red tips like the finger-points of two fairy hands, tenderly joined together, pointed up in little cones to keep the yellow stars warm within, that they might shine bright when the great star of day came to look for them.

Alec Forbes of Howglen

THE MINISTRY OF NATURE

The best thing you can do for your fellow, next to rousing his conscience, is — not to give him things to think about, but to wake things up that are in him, or say, to make him think things for himself. The best Nature does for us is to work in us such moods in which thoughts of high import arise. Does any aspect of Nature wake but one thought? Does she ever suggest one definite thing? Does she make any two men in the same place at the same moment think the same thing? Is she therefore a failure, because she is not definite? Is it nothing that she rouses the something deeper than the understanding — the power that underlies thoughts? Does she not set feeling, and so thinking at work? Would it be better that she did this thing after one fashion and not after many fashions? Nature is mood-engendering, thought-provoking; such ought the sonata, such ought the fairytale to be.

A Dish of Orts

62

RELIGION AND BEAUTY

One of my greatest difficulties in consenting to think of religion was that I thought I should have to give up my beautiful thoughts and my love for the things

God has made. But I find that the happiness springing from all things not in themselves sinful is much increased by religion. God is the God of the Beautiful — Religion is the love of the Beautiful, and Heaven is the Home of the Beautiful — Nature is tenfold brighter in the Sun of Righteousness, and my love of Nature is more intense since I became a Christian — if indeed I am one. God has not given me such thoughts and forbidden me to enjoy them.

from a letter

63
INFLUENCES

It is not necessary that the intellect should define and separate before the heart and soul derive nourishment. As well say that a bee can get nothing out of a flower, because she does not understand botany. The very music of the stately words of such a poem [Milton's *Comus*] is enough to generate a better mood, to make one feel the air of higher regions, and wish to rise 'above the smoke and stir of this dim spot'. The best influences which bear upon us are of this vague sort — powerful upon the heart and conscience, although undefined to the intellect.

Ranald Bannerman's Boyhood

LONGING

O God of mountains, stars, and boundless spaces,
O God of freedom and of joyous hearts,
When thy face looketh forth from all men's faces,
There will be room enough in crowded marts!
Brood thou around me, and the noise is o'er,
Thy universe my closet with shut door.

Poetical Works

65

WE MAKE

We make, but thou art the creating core.
Whatever thing I dream, invent, or feel,
Thou art the heart of it, the atmosphere,
Thou art inside all love man ever bore.

Diary of an Old Soul

Either there is a God, and that God the perfect heart of truth and loveliness, or all poetry and art is but an unsown, unplanted, unrooted flower, crowning a somewhat symmetrical heap of stones. The man who sees no beauty in its petals, finds no perfume in its breath, may well accord it the parentage of the stones; the man whose heart swells beholding it will be ready to think it has roots that reach below them.

Thomas Wingfold, Curate

The worshippers of science will themselves allow, that when they cannot gain observations enough to satisfy them upon any point in which a law of nature is involved, they must, if possible, institute experiments. I say therefore to those whose observation has not satisfied them concerning the phenomenon of Christianity — 'Where is your experiment? Why do you not thus try the utterance claiming to be the law of life? Call it a hypothesis, and experiment upon it. Carry into practice, well justified of your conscience, the words which the Man spoke, for therein he says himself lies the possibility of your acceptance of his mission; and if, after reasonable time thus spent, you are not yet convinced enough to give testimony — I will not annoy you by saying *to facts*, but — to conviction, I think neither will you be ready to abandon the continuous experiment.'

England's Antiphon

POOR CRITICS

It is not the man who knows most about Nature that is hardest to please, however he may be the hardest to satisfy, with the attempt to follow her. The accomplished poet will derive pleasure from verses which are a mockery to the soul of the unhappy mortal whose business is judgement — the most thankless of all labours, and justly so. Certain fruits one is unable to like until he has eaten them in their perfection; after that, the reminder in them of the perfect will enable him to enjoy even the inferior a little, recognizing their kind — always provided he be not one given to judgement — a connoisseur, that is, or who cares less for the truth than for the knowing comparison of one embodiment of it with another.

Sir Gibbie

69

EYES MADE FOR GLORY

That thou are nowhere to be found, agree
Wise men, whose eyes are but for surfaces;
Men with eyes opened by the second birth,
To whom the seen, husk of the unseen is,
Descry thee soul of everything on earth.
Who know thy ends, thy means and motions see;
Eyes made for glory soon discover thee.

Diary of an Old Soul

'I do wish, my lady' said Donal, 'you would not sit so much where there is little sunlight! Outer and inner things are in their original one; the light of the sun is the natural world-clothing of the truth, and whoever sits much in the physical dark misses a great help to understanding the things of the light. If I were your director,' he went on, 'I would counsel you to change this room for one with a broad, fair outlook; so that, when gloomy thoughts hid God from you, they might have his eternal contradiction in the face of his heaven and earth.'

Donal Grant

71

MAGIC MIRRORS

Why are all reflections lovelier than what we call the reality? — not so grand or strong, it may be, but always lovelier? Fair as is the gliding sloop on the shining sea, the wavering, trembling, unresting sail below is fairer still. Yea, the reflecting ocean itself, reflected in the mirror, has a wondrousness about its waters that somewhat vanishes when I turn towards itself. All mirrors are magic mirrors. The commonest room is a room in a poem when I turn to the glass . . . In whatever way it may be accounted for, of one thing we may be sure, that this feeling is no cheat; for there is no cheating in Nature and the simple unsought feelings of the soul. There must be a truth involved in it, though we may but in part lay hold of the meaning. Even the memories of past pain are beautiful; and past delights, though beheld only through clefts in the grey clouds of sorrow, are lovely as Fairy Land.

Phantastes

BEAUTY

All lovely sights tend to keep the soul pure, to lift the heart up to God, and above, not merely what people call low cares, but what people would call reasonable cares, although our great Teacher teaches us that such cares are unjust towards our Father in Heaven. More than that, by helping to keep the mind calm and pure, they help to keep the imagination, which is the source of all invention, active, and the judgement, which weighs all its suggestions, just. Whatever is beautiful is of God, and it is only ignorance or a low condition of heart and soul that does not prize what is beautiful.

Gutta Percha Willie

WIND OF GOD

O wind of God, that bloweth in the mind,
Blow, blow and wake the gentle spring in me;
Blow, swifter blow, a strong warm summer wind,
Till all the flowers with eyes come out to see;
Blow till the fruit hangs red on every tree,
And our high-soaring song-larks meet thy dove —
High the imperfect soars, descends the perfect dove!

Blow not the less though winter cometh then;
Blow, wind of God, blow hither changes keen;
Let the spring creep into the ground again,
The flowers close all their eyes and not be seen:
All lives in thee that ever once hath been!
Blow, fill my upper air with icy storms;
Breathe cold, O wind of God, and kill my canker-
worms.

Poetical Works

This world looks to us the natural and simple one, and so it is — absolutely fitted to our need and education. But there is that in us which is not at home in this world, which I believe holds secret relations with every star, or perhaps rather, with that in the heart of God whence issued every star, diverse in kind and character as in colour and place and motion and light. To that in us, this world is so far strange and unnatural and unfitting, and we need a yet homelier home. Yea, no home at last will do, but the home of God's heart.

Thomas Wingfold, Curate

The highest poetic feeling of which we are not conscious, springs not from the beholding of perfected beauty, but from the mute sympathy which the creation with all its children manifests with us in the groaning and travailing which look for the sonship. Because of our need and aspiration, the snowdrop gives birth in our hearts to a loftier spiritual and poetic feeling, than the rose most complete in form, colour and odour. The rose is of Paradise — the snowdrop is of the striving, hoping, longing Earth. Perhaps our highest poetry is the expression of our aspirations in the sympathetic forms of visible Nature. Nor is this merely a longing for a restored Paradise; for even in the ordinary history of men, no man or woman that has fallen can be restored to the position formerly held. Such must rise to a yet higher place, whence they can behold their former standing far beneath their feet. They must be restored by the attainment of something better than they ever possessed before, or not at all. If the law be a weariness, we must escape it by taking refuge with the spirit, for not otherwise can we fulfil the law than by being above the law.

Adela Cathcart

There is one truth about a plain face, that may not have occurred to many: its ugliness accompanies a condition of larger undevelopment, for all ugliness that is not evil, is undevelopment; and so implies the larger material and possibility of development. The idea of no countenance is yet carried out, and this kind will take more developing for the completion of its idea, and may result in a greater beauty. I would therefore advise any young man of aspiration in the matter of beauty, to choose a plain woman for wife — if through her plainness she is yet lovely in his eyes; for the loveliness is herself, victorious over the plainness, and her face, so far from complete and yet serving her loveliness, has in it room for completion on a grander scale than possibly more handsome faces. In a handsome face one sees the lines of its coming perfection, and has a glimpse of what it must be when finished; few are prophets enough for a plain face. A keen surprise of beauty awaits many a man if he be pure enough to come near the transfiguration of the homely face he loved.

What's Mine's Mine

INDIVIDUALS

As the fir tree lifts up itself with a far different need from the need of the palm-tree, so does each man stand before God, and lift up a different humanity to the common Father. And for each God has a different response.

Unspoken Sermons

78

UNIQUENESS

Crossing the wide space where so lately they had burned the heather that the sheep might have its young shoots in the spring, the brothers stood, and gazed around with delight.

'There is nothing like this anywhere!' said Ian.

'Do you mean nothing so beautiful?' asked Alister.

'No, I mean just what I say: there is nothing like it. I do not care a straw whether one scene be more or less beautiful than another; what I do care for is — its individual speech to my soul. I feel towards visions of Nature as towards writers. If a book or a prospect produces in my mind a mood that no other produces, then I feel it individual, original, real, therefore precious. If a scene or a song play upon the organ of my heart as no other scene or song could, why should I ask at all whether it be beautiful? A bare hill may be more to me than a garden of Damascus but I love them both. The first question as to any work of art is whether it puts the willing soul into any mood at all peculiar; the second, what that mood is. It matters to me little by whom our Ossian was composed, and it matters nothing whoever in his ignorance may declare that there never was an Ossian any more than a Homer: here is a something that has power over my heart and soul, works upon them as nothing else does. I do not ask whether its power be great or small; it is enough that it is a peculiar power, one by itself; that it puts my spiritual consciousness in a certain individual condition, such in character as nothing else can occasion. Either a man or a nation must have felt it to make me so feel.'

What's Mine's Mine

79
THE TWO FIRES OF GOD

The earth is like a man: the great glowing fire is God in the heart of the earth, and the great sun is God in the sky, keeping it warm on the other side. Our gladness and pleasure, our trouble when we do wrong, our love for all about us, that is God inside us; and the beautiful things and lovable people, and all the lessons of life in history and poetry, in the Bible, and in whatever comes to us, is God outside of us. Every life is between two great fires of the love of God.

Donal Grant

[Cosmo] came to the spot where his father and he had prayed together, and there kneeling lifted up his face to the stars. Oh mighty, only church! whose roof is a vaulted infinitude! whose lights come burning from the maker! Church of all churches — where the Son of Man prayed! In the narrow temple of Herod he taught the people, and out of it drove the dishonest traders; but here, under the starry roof, was his house of prayer! Church where is not a mark of human hand! church that is all church and nothing but church, built without hands, despised and desecrated more by unbelief than by any sin! church of God's own building! thou alone in thy grandeur art fitting type of a yet greater, a yet holier, yea the one real church, whose stars are the burning eyes of unutterable, self-forgetting love, whose worship is a ceaseless ministration of self-forgetting deeds — the one real ideal church, the body of the living Christ, compact of the hearts and souls of men and women of every nation and every creed through all time and over all the world — redeemed alike from Judaism, paganism, and all the self-asserting Christianities that darken and dishonour the self-forgetting Christ, and growing together in him to one great God-reflecting family of the living Father!

Castle Warlock

HOME

What a word *home* is! To think that God has made the world so that you have only to be born in a certain place, and live long enough in it to get at the secret of it, and henceforth that place is to you a *home* with all the wonderful meaning in the word. Thus the whole earth is a home for the race; for every spot of it shares in the feeling: some one of the family loves it as *his* home.

The Seaboard Parish

NOTHING IS ALIEN

Nothing is alien in thy world immense —
No look of sky or earth or man or beast;
'In the great hand of God I stand, and thence
Look out on life, his endless, holy feast.
To try to feel is but to court despair,
To dig for a sun within a garden-fence:
Who does thy will, O God, he lives upon thy air.'

Poetical Works

MAN AND THE WORLD

There is yet a higher and more sustained influence exercised by Nature, and that takes effect when she puts a man into that mood or condition in which thoughts come of themselves. That is perhaps the best thing that can be done for us, the best at least that Nature can do. It is certainly higher than mere intellectual teaching . . . If the world proceeded from the imagination of God, and man proceeded from the love of God, it is easy to believe that that which proceeded from the imagination of God should rouse the best thoughts in the mind of a being who proceeded from the love of God. This I think is the relation between man and the world.

A Dish of Orts

❁

I do not think this mood, wherein all forms of beauty sped to his soul as to their own needful centre, could have lasted over many miles of his journey. But such delicate inward revelations are none the less precious that they are evanescent. Many feelings are simply too good to last — using the phrase not in the unbelieving sense in which it is generally used, expressing the conviction that God is a hard father, fond of disappointing his children, but to express the fact that intensity and endurance cannot yet coexist in the human economy. But the virtue of a mood depends by no means on its immediate presence. Like any other experience, it may be believed in, and, in the absence which leaves the mind free to contemplate it, works even more good than in its presence.

Robert Falconer

I can no more describe the emotion aroused in my mind by a gray cloud parting over a gray stone, by the smell of a sweet-pea, by the sight of one of those long upright pennons of striped grass with the homely name, than I can tell what the glory of God is who made these things. The Man whose poetry is like Nature in this, that it produces individual, incommunicable moods and conditions of mind — a sense of elevated, tender, marvellous, and evanescent existence, must be a poet indeed. Every dawn of such a feeling is a light-brushed bubble rendering visible for a moment the dark unknown sea of our being which lies beyond the lights of our consciousness, and is the stuff and region of our eternal growth. But think what language must become before it will tell dreams! — before it will convey the delicate shades of fancy that come and go in the brain of a child! — before it will let a man know wherein one face differeth from another face in glory! I suspect, however, that for such purposes it is rather music than articulation that is needful — that, with a hope of these finer results, the language must rather be turned into music than logically extended.

Robert Falconer

No revelation can be other than partial. If for true revelation a man must be told all the truth, then farewell to revelation; yea, farewell to the sonship. For what revelation, other than a partial, can the highest spiritual condition receive of the infinite God? But it is not therefore untrue because it is partial . . . Only if its nature were such as to preclude development and growth, thus chaining a man to its incompleteness, it would be but a false revelation fighting against all the divine laws of human existence. The true revelation rouses the desire to know more by the truth of its incompleteness.

Unspoken Sermons

THE SOUL'S GROWTH

There is the still growth of the moonlit night of reverie; cloudy, with wind, and a little rain, comes the morning of thought, when the mind grows faster and the heart more slowly, then wakes the storm in the forest of human relation, tempest and lightning abroad, the soul enlarging by great bursts of vision and leaps of understanding and resolve; then floats up the mystic twilight eagerness, not unmingled with the dismay of compelled progress, when, bidding farewell to that which is behind, the soul is driven toward that which is before, grasping at it with all the hunger of the new birth. The story of God's universe lies in the growth of the individual soul.

Heather and Snow

DIVINE CHILDHOOD

God is represented in Jesus, for that God is like Jesus: Jesus is represented in the child, for that Jesus is like the child. Therefore God is represented in the child, for that he is like the child. God is childlike. In the true vision of this fact lies the receiving of God in the child . . . Our Lord became flesh, but did not *become* man. He took on him the form of a man: he was man already. He could never have been a child if he would ever have ceased to be a child, for in him the transient found nothing. Childhood belongs to the divine nature.

Unspoken Sermons

89
TRUE BRAVERY

'But I wasn't brave of myself,' said Diamond, whom my older readers will have already discovered to be a true child in this, that he was given to metaphysics. 'It was the wind that blew in my face that made me brave. Wasn't it now, North Wind?'

'Yes: I know that. You had to be taught what courage was. And you couldn't know what it was without feeling it: therefore it was given you. But don't you feel as if you would try to be brave yourself next time?'

'Yes, I do. But trying is not much.'

'Yes, it is — a very great deal, for it is a beginning. And a beginning is the greatest thing of all. To try to be brave is to be brave. The coward who tries to be brave is before the man who is brave because he is made so, and never had to try.'

At the Back of the North Wind

Many things were spoken by the simple wisdom of David, which would have enlightened Hugh far more than they did, had he been sufficiently advanced to receive them. But their very simplicity was often far beyond the grasp of his thoughts; for the higher we rise, the simpler we become; and David was one of those of whom is the kingdom of Heaven. There is a childhood into which we have to grow, just as there is a childhood which we must leave behind; a childlikeness which is the highest gain of humanity, and a childishness from which but a few of those who are counted the wisest among men, have freed themselves in their imagined progress towards the reality of things.

David Elginbrod

'What would you have done with [the child]? Got it into some orphan asylum? — or the Foundling perhaps?'

'Never,' Falconer answered. 'All these societies are wretched inventions for escape from the right way. There ought not to be an orphan asylum in the kingdom.'

'What! Would you put them all down, then?'

'God forbid! But I would, if I could, make them all useless.'

'How would you do that?'

'I would *merely* enlighten the hearts of childless people as to their privileges.'

'Which are?'

'To be fathers and mothers to the fatherless and motherless.'

'I have often wondered why more of them did not adopt children. Why don't they?'

'For various reasons which a real love to child nature would blow to the winds — all comprised in this, that such a child would not be their own child. As if ever a child could be their own! That a child is God's is of rather more consequence than whether it is born of this or that couple. Their hearts would surely be glad when they went into heaven to have the angels of the little ones that always behold the face of their Father coming round them, though they were not exactly their father and mother.'

Robert Falconer

Mary, to thee the heart was given
For infant hand to hold,
And clasp thus, an eternal heaven,
The great earth in its fold.

He seized the world with tender might
By making thee his own;
Thee lowly queen, whose heavenly height
Was to thyself unknown.

He came, all helpless, to thy power,
For warmth, and love, and birth;
In thy embraces, every hour,
He grew into the earth.

Poetical Works

THAT HOLY THING

They all were looking for a king
To slay their foes, and lift them high:
Thou cam'st a little baby thing
That made a woman cry.

O Son of Man, to right my lot
Nought but thy presence can avail;
Yet on the road Thy wheels are not,
Nor on the sea Thy sail!

My fancied ways why should'st Thou heed?
Thou com'st down Thine own secret stair;
Com'st down to answer all my need,
Yea, every bygone prayer!

Poetical Works

The winter is the childhood of the year. Into this childhood of the year came the child Jesus; and into this childhood of the year must we all descend. It is as if God spoke to each of us according to our need: My son, my daughter, you are growing old and cunning; you must grow a child again, with my son, this blessed birth-time. You are growing old and careful; you must become a child. You are growing old and distrustful; you must become a child. You are growing old and petty, and weak and foolish; you must become a child — my child, like the baby there, that strong sunrise of faith and hope and love, lying in his mother's arms in the stable.

Adela Cathcart

TRUE DREAMS

Seek not that your sons and your daughters should not see visions, should not dream dreams; seek that they should see true visions, that they should dream noble dreams. Such out-going of the imagination is one with aspiration, and will do more to elevate above what is low and vile than all possible inculcations of morality.

A Dish of Orts

GOD'S HEIRS

But all things shall be ours! Up, heart, and sing
All things were made for us — we are God's heirs —
Moon, sun, and wildest comets that do trail
A crowd of small worlds for a swiftness-tail!
Up from thy depths in me, my child-heart bring —
The child alone inherits anything:
God's little children-gods — all things are theirs!

Diary of an Old Soul

Diamond's father and mother were, notwithstanding, rather miserable, and Diamond began to feel a kind of darkness beginning to spread over his own mind. But the same moment he said to himself: 'This will never do. I can't give in to this. I've been to the back of the North Wind. Things go right there, and so I must try to get things to go right here. I've got to fight the miserable things. They shan't make me miserable if I can help it.' I do not mean that he thought these very words. They are perhaps too grown-up for him to have thought, but they represent the kind of thing that was in his heart and his head. And when heart and head go together, nothing can stand before them ... Thereupon Diamond thought it time that somebody did something, and as himself was the only somebody at hand, he must go and see whether he could not do the something ... Now the way most people do when they see anything very miserable is to turn away from the sight, and try to forget it. But Diamond began as usual to try to destroy the misery. The little boy was just as much one of God's messengers as if he had been an angel with a flaming sword, going out to fight the devil. The devil he had to fight just then was Misery.

At the Back of the North Wind

It had been a very small grumble, but there are no sins for which there is less reason or less excuse than small ones: in no sense are they worth committing. And we grown people commit many more such than little children, and have our reward in childishness instead of childlikeness.

Donal Grant

The child's fear of rats amounted to a frenzied horror. She dared not move a finger. To get out of bed with those creatures running about the room was as impossible as it was to cry out. But her heart did what her tongue could not do — cried out with a great and bitter cry to one who was more ready to hear than Robert and Nancy Bruce. And what her heart cried was this:

'O God, tak' care o' me frae the rottans.'

There was no need to send an angel from heaven in answer to this little one's prayer: the cat would do. Annie heard a scratch and a mew at the door. The rats made one frantic scramble, and were still.

'It's pussy!' she cried, recovering the voice for joy that had failed her for fear.

Fortified by her arrival, and still more by the feeling that she was a divine messenger sent to succour her because she had prayed, she sprang out of bed, darted across the room, and opened the door to let her in. A few moments and she was fast asleep, guarded by God's angel, the cat, for whose entrance she took good care ever after to leave the door ajar.

There are ways of keeping the door of the mind also, ready as it is to fall to, ajar for the cat.

Alec Forbes of Howglen

I have no choice, I must do what I can;
But thou dost me, and all things else as well;
Thou wilt take care thy child shall grow a man.
Rouse thee, my faith; be king; with life be one;
To trust in God is action's highest kind;
Who trusts in God, his heart with life doth swell;
Faith opens all the windows to God's wind.

Diary of an Old Soul

101
OTHER-WORLDLINESS

The childlike, the essential, the divine notion of serving, with their everyday will and being, the will of the
living one, who lived for them that they might live, as
once he had died for them that they might die, rip-
ened in them to a Christianity that saw God everywhere, saw that everything had to be done as God
would have it done, and that nothing but injustice had
to be forsaken to please him. They were under no
influence of what has been so well called *other-
worldliness*; for they saw this world as much God's as
that, saw that its work has to be done divinely, that it
is the beginning of the world to come. It was to them
all one world, with God in it, all in all; therefore the
best work for the other world, was the work of this
world.

The Elect Lady

IN THE GUTTER

I see a little child whose eager hands
Search the thick stream that drains the crowded
  street
For possible things hid in its current slow.
Near by, behind him, a great palace stands,
Where kings might welcome nobles to their feet.
Soft sounds, sweet scents, fair sights there only go —
There the child's father lives, but the child does not
  know.

Diary of an Old Soul

WIDE LOVE

A man must learn to love his children not because
they are his, but because they are *children*, else his
love will be scarcely a better thing at last than the
party-spirit of the faithful politician. I doubt if it will
prove even so good a thing.

Alec Forbes of Howglen

POOR SUBSTITUTE

It is the need of a child that makes so many women take to poor, miserable, broken-nosed lap-dogs; for they are self-indulgent, and cannot face the troubles and dangers of adopting a child. They would if they might get one of a good family, or from a respectable home; but they dare not take an orphan out of the dirt, lest it should spoil their silken chairs.

The Seaboard Parish

FOOLISH CAUTION

I am a fool when I would stop and think,
And, lest I lose my thoughts, from duty shrink.
It is but avarice in another shape.
'Tis as the vine branch were to hoard the grape,
Nor trust the living root beneath the sod.
What trouble is that child to thee, my God.
Who sips thy gracious cup, and will not drink!

Diary of an Old Soul

Could Diamond have had greater praise or greater pleasure? You see, when he forgot his Self his mother took care of his Self, and loved and praised his Self. Our own praises poison our Selves, and puff and swell them up, till they lose all shape and beauty, and become like great toadstools. But the praises of father or mother do our Selves good, and comfort them and make them beautiful. *They* never do them any harm. If they do any harm, it comes of mixing some of our own praises with them, and that turns them nasty and slimy and poisonous.

At the Back of the North Wind

A PRAYER

When I look back upon my life nigh spent,
Nigh spent, although the stream as yet flows on,
I more of follies than of sins repent,
Less for offence than Love's shortcomings moan.
With self, O Father, leave me not alone —
Leave not with the beguiler the beguiled;
Besmirched and ragged, Lord, take back thine own:
A fool I bring thee, to be made a child.

Poetical Works

GOD IN MAN

When the human soul is not yet able to receive the vision of the God-man, God sometimes — might I not say always — reveals himself, or at least gives himself in some human being whose face, whose hands are the ministering angels of his unacknowledged presence, to keep alive the fire of love on the altar of the heart.

Robert Falconer

The love of God is the soul of Christianity. Christ is the body of that truth. The love of God is the creating and redeeming, the forming and satisfying power of the universe. The love of God is that which kills evil and glorifies goodness. It is the safety of the great whole. It is the home-atmosphere of all life. Well does the poet of the 'Christmas Eve' say :—

> *'The loving worm within its clod,*
> *Were diviner than a loveless God*
> *Amid his worlds, I will dare to say.'*

Surely, then, inasmuch as man is made in the image of God, nothing less than a love in the image of God's love, all-embracing, quietly excusing, heartily commending, can constitute the blessedness of man ; a love not insensible to that which is foreign to it, but overcoming it with good. Where man loves in his kind, even as God loves in His kind, then man is saved, then he has reached the unseen and eternal . . . We must wait patiently for the completion of God's great harmony, and meantime love everywhere and as we can.

A Dish of Orts

That our Lord meant by the love of our neighbour, not the fulfilling of the law towards him, but that condition of being which results in the fulfilling of the law and more, is sufficiently clear from his story of the good Samaritan. 'Who is my neighbour?' said the lawyer. And the Lord taught him that everyone to whom he could be or for whom he could do anything was his neighbour; therefore, that each of the race, as he comes within the touch of one tentacle of our nature, is our neighbour. Which of the inhibitions of the law is illustrated in the tale? Not one. The love that is more than law, and renders its breach impossible, lives in the endless story, coming out in active kindness, that is, the recognition of kin, of *kind*, of nighness, of *neighbourhood*; yea in tenderness and loving-kindness — the Samaritan-heart akin to the Jew-heart, the Samaritan hands neighbours to the Jewish wounds.

Unspoken Sermons

LOVE IS STRENGTH

Love alone is great in might,
Makes the heavy burden light,
Smooths rough ways to weary feet,
Makes the bitter morsel sweet:
Love alone is strength!

Might that is not born of Love
Is not Might born from above,
Has its birthplace down below
Where they neither reap nor sow:
Love alone is strength!

Love is stronger than all force,
In its own eternal source;
Might is always in decay,
Love grows fresher every day.
Love alone is strength!

Little ones, no ill can chance;
Fear ye not, but sing and dance;
Though the high-heaved heaven should fall
God is plenty for us all:
God is Love and Strength!

Poetical Works

'It would be so nice to be able to do everything!' said Willie.

'So it would; but nobody can; and it's just as well, for then we should not need so much help from each other, and would be too independent.'

'Then shouldn't a body try to do as many things as he can?'

'Yes, for there's no fear of ever being able to do without other people, and you would be so often able to help them. Both the smith and the watchmaker could mend a lock, but neither of them could do without the other for all that.'

Gutta Percha Willie

AN OPEN HEART

Make not thy heart a casket.
Opening seldom, quick to close;
But of bread a wide-mouthed basket,
Or a cup that overflows.

Poetical Works

SHARING BURDENS

'My dear boy, persons who are so near each other as we are, must not only bear the consequences together of any wrong done by one of them, but must, in a sense, bear each other's iniquities even. If I sin, you must suffer; if you sin, you being my own boy, I must suffer. But this is not all: it lies upon both of us to do what we can to get rid of the wrong done; and thus we have to bear each other's sin. I am accountable to make amends as far as I can and also to do what I can to get you to be sorry and make amends as far as you can.'

'But papa, isn't that hard?' I asked.

'Do you think I should like to leave you to get out of your sin as you best could, or sink deeper and deeper into it? Should I grudge anything to take the weight of the sin, or the wrong to others, off you? Do you think I should want not to be troubled about it? Or if I were to do anything wrong, would you think it very hard that you had to help me to be good, and set things right? Even if people looked down upon you because of me, would you say it was hard? Would you not rather say, "I'm glad to bear anything for my father: I'll share with him?"'

'Yes, indeed, papa. I would rather share with you than not, whatever it was.'

'Then you see, my boy, how kind God is in tying us up in one bundle that way. It is a grand and beautiful thing that the fathers should suffer for the children, and the children for the fathers.'

Ranald Bannerman's Boyhood

115
BROTHERHOOD

The ancient clan-feeling is good in this, that it opens a channel whose very existence is a justification for the flow of simple human feelings along all possible levels of social position. And I would there were more of it. Only something better is coming instead of it — a recognition of the infinite brotherhood in Christ. All other relations, all attempts by churches, by associations, by secret societies — of Freemasons and others, are good merely as they tend to destroy themselves in the wider truth; as they teach men to be dissatisfied with their limitations.

Robert Falconer

TRUE WOMEN

In the real world, there are no ladies but true women. Also they only are beautiful. All there show what they are, and the others are all more or less deformed. Oh! what lovely ladies will walk into the next world out of the rough cocoon of their hard-wrought bodies — not because they have been working women, but because they have been true women. Among working women as among countesses, there are last that shall be first and first that shall be last. *What kind of women* will be the question.

There and Back

LOVE IS THE PART

Love is the part, and love is the whole,
Love is the robe, and love is the pall;
Ruler of heart and brain and soul,
Love is the lord and the slave of all!
I thank thee, Love, that I love thee;
I thank thee more that thou lov'st me.

Poetical Works

NO CHOICE OF NEIGHBOUR

A man must not choose his neighbour; he must take the neighbour that God sends him. In him, whoever he be, lies, hidden or revealed, a beautiful brother. A neighbour is just the man who is next to you at the moment, the man with whom any business has brought you in contact.

Thus will love spread and spread in wider and stronger pulses till the whole human race will be to the man sacredly lovely. Drink-debased, vice-disfigured, pride-puffed, wealth-bollen, vanity-smeared, they will yet be brothers, yet be sisters, yet be God-born neighbours.

Unspoken Sermons

THE PERFECTING OF LOVES

I do not mean that God would have even his closest presence make us forget or cease to desire that of our friend. God forbid! The love of God is the perfecting of every love. He is not the God of oblivion, but of eternal remembrance. There is no past with him. So far is he from such jealousy as we have all heard imputed to him, his determination is that his sons and daughters shall love each other perfectly. He gave us to each other to belong to each other for ever.

Unspoken Sermons

THE EYES OF LOVE

Love is the rain, and love is the air,
Love is the earth that holdeth fast;
Love is the root that is buried there,
Love is the open flower at last!
I thank thee, Love all round about,
That the eyes of my love are looking out.

Poetical Works

LONELINESS

The sense of loneliness seized upon me, and the first sense of absolute loneliness is awful. Independent as a man may fancy himself in the heart of a world of men, he is only to be convinced that there is neither voice nor hearing, to know that the face from which he most recoils is of a kind essential to his very soul. Space is not room; and when we complain of the overcrowding of our fellows, we are thankless for that which comforts us the most, and desire its absence in ignorance of our deepest nature.

William Cumbermede

MERCY

The demand for mercy is far from being for the sake only of the man who needs his neighbour's mercy; it is greatly more for the sake of the man who must show the mercy. It is a small thing to a man whether or not his neighbour be merciful to him; it is life or death to him whether or not he be merciful to his neighbour . . . The reward of the merciful is, that by their mercy they are rendered capable of receiving the mercy of God — yea God himself, who is Mercy.

The Hope of the Gospel

LOVE OF WOMAN

The man who throughly loves God and his neighbour is the only man who will love a woman ideally — who can love her with the love God thought of between them when he made man male and female. The man, I repeat, who loves God with his very life, and his neighbour as Christ loves him, is the man who alone is capable of grand, perfect, glorious love to any woman.

Sir Gibbie

THE CURE IS LOVE

Alas, how easily things go wrong!
A sigh too much, or a kiss too long,
And there follows a mist and a weeping rain,
And life is never the same again . . . .

But what is left for the cold gray soul,
That moans like a wounded dove?
One wine is left in the broken bowl —
'Tis — to love, and love, and love.

Better to sit at the water's birth,
Than a sea of waves to win;
To live in the love that floweth forth,
Than the love that cometh in.

Be thy heart a well of love, my child,
Flowing, and free, and sure;
For a cistern of love, though undefiled,
Keeps not the spirit pure.

Phantastes

A WORLD OF MEN

So superbly constituted, so simply complicate is man; he rises from and stands upon such a pedestal of lower physical organisms and spiritual structures, that no atmosphere will comfort or nourish his life, less divine than that offered by other souls; nowhere but in other lives can he ripen his specialty, develop the idea of himself, the individuality that distinguishes him from every other. Were all men alike, each would still have an individuality, secured by his personal consciousness, but there would be small reason why there should be more than two or three such; while for the development of the differences which make a large and lofty unit possible, and which alone can make millions into a church, an endless and measureless influence and reaction are indispensible. A man to be perfect — complete, that is, in having reached the spiritual condition of persistent and universal growth, which is the mode wherein he inherits the infinitude of the Father — must have the education of a world of fellow men.

Lilith

126
IMPERFECT HUMANITY

It is the mark of an imperfect humanity, that personal knowledge should spur the sides of hospitable intent: what difference does our knowing or not knowing make to the fact of human need? The good Samaritan would never have been mentioned by the mouth of the True, had he been even an old acquaintance of the 'certain man'. But it is thus we learn; and from loving this one and that, we come to love all at last, and then is our humanity complete.

Mary Marston

LOVE IS THE SUN

Love is the sun, and love is the sea;
Love is the tide that comes and goes;
Flowing and flowing it comes to me;
Ebbing and ebbing to thee it flows!
Oh my sun, and my wind, and tide!
My sea, and my shore, and all beside!

Poetical Works

A GOOD MOTHER

Mrs Peterson was such a nice good mother! All mothers are nice and good more or less, but Mrs Peterson was nice and good all *more* and no *less*. She made and kept a little heaven in that poor cottage on the high hill-side — for her husband and son to go home to out of the low and rather dreary earth in which they worked. I doubt if the princess was very much happier even in the arms of her huge-great-grandmother than Peter and Curdie were in the arms of Mrs Peterson. True, her hands were hard and chapped and large, but it was with work for them; and therefore in the sight of the angels, her hands were so much the more beautiful. And if Curdie worked hard to get her a petticoat, she worked hard every day to get him comforts which he would have missed much more than she would a new petticoat even in winter. Not that she and Curdie ever thought of how much they worked for each other: that would have spoiled everything.

The Princess and the Goblin

LOVE AND TRUTH

Love is the first comforter, and where love and truth speak, the love will be felt where the truth is never perceived. Love indeed is the highest of all truth; and the pressure of a hand, a kiss, the caress of a child, will do more to save sometimes, than the wisest argument, even rightly understood. Love alone is wisdom, love alone is power; and where love seems to fail, it is where self has stepped between and dulled the potency of its rays.

Paul Faber, Surgeon

I knew now, that it is by loving, and not by being loved, that one can come nearest the soul of another; yea, that, where two love, it is the loving of each other, and not the being beloved by each other, that originates and perfects and assures their blessedness. I knew that love gives to him that loveth, power over any soul beloved, even if that soul know him not, bringing him inwardly close to that spirit; a power that cannot be but for good; for in proportion as selfishness intrudes, the love ceases, and the power that springs therefrom dies. Yet all love will, one day, meet with its return. All true love will, one day, behold its own image in the eyes of the beloved, and be humbly glad.

Phantastes

Dost thou ever feel thus toward thy neighbour —
'Yes, of course, every man is my brother; but how
can I be a brother to him so long as he thinks me
wrong in what I believe, and so long as I think he
wrongs in his opinions the dignity of the truth?'
What, I return, has the man no hand to grasp, no eyes
into which yours may gaze far deeper than your
vaunted intellect can follow? Is there not, I ask, anything in him to love? Who asks you to be of one
opinion? It is the Lord who asks you to be of one
heart. Does the Lord love the man? Can the Lord
love, where there is nothing to love? Are you wiser
than he, inasmuch as you perceive impossibility
where he has failed to discover it? . . . Let it humble
thee to know that thy dearest opinion, the one thou
dost worship as if it, and not God, were thy Saviour,
this very opinion thou art doomed to change, for it
cannot possibly be right, if it work in thee for death
and not for life.

A Dish of Orts

'You never made that song, Diamond,' said his
mother.

'No, Mother. I wish I had. No I don't. That would

be to take it from somebody else. But it's mine for all that.'

'What makes it yours?'

'I love it so.'

'Does loving a thing make it yours?'

'I think so, Mother — at least more than anything else can. If I didn't love baby (which couldn't be, you know), she wouldn't be mine a bit. But I do love baby, and baby is my very own Dulcimer.'

'The baby's mine, Diamond.'

'That makes her the more mine, Mother.'

'How do you make that out?'

'Because you're mine, Mother.'

'Is that because you love me?'

'Yes, just because. Love makes the only myness,' said Diamond.

At the Back of the North Wind

133
'DEAR JESUS'

I have read a story somewhere of a poor child that dropped a letter into the post-office, addressed to 'Jesus Christ in Heaven'. And it reached him, and the child had her answer. For was it not Christ present in the good man or woman — I forget the particulars of the story — who sent the child the help she needed?

David Elginbrod

Mrs Wingfold had developed a great faculty for liking people. It was quite a fresh shoot of her nature, for she had before been rather of a repellent disposition. I wish there were more, and amongst them some of the best people, similarly changed. Surely the latter soon would be, if once they had a glimpse of how much the coming of the kingdom is retarded by defect of courtesy. The people I mean are slow to *like*, and until they come to *like*, they *seem* to dislike. I have known such whose manner was fit to imply entire disapprobation of the very existence of those upon whom they looked for the first time. They might then have been saying to themselves, 'I would never have created such people!' Had I not known them, I could not have imagined them lovers of God or man, though they were of both. True courtesy, that is, courtesy born of a true heart, is a most lovely, and absolutely indispensible grace — one that nobody but a Christian can thoroughly develop. God grant us a 'coming-on disposition', as Shakespeare calls it.

Paul Faber, Surgeon

O God of man, my heart would worship all
My fellow men, the flashes from thy fire;
Them in good sooth my lofty kindred call,
Born of the same one heart, the perfect sire,
Love of my kind alone can set me free;
Help me to welcome all that come to me,
Not close my doors and dream solitude liberty!

Diary of an Old Soul

136
EXPANDING LOVE

'We have even got to feel a man is our brother the moment we see him,' pursued Donal, enhancing his former remark.

'That sounds alarming!' said Miss Graeme, with another laugh. 'My little heart feels not large enough to receive so many.'

'The worst of it is,' continued Donal, who once started was not ready to draw rein, 'that those who chiefly advocate this extension of the family bonds, begin by loving their own immediate relations less than anybody else. Extension with them means slackening — as if anyone could learn to love more by loving less, or go on to do better without doing well! He who loves his own little will not love others much.'

Donal Grant

MEDDLING

In his inmost being he knew that the mission of man is to help his neighbour. But in as much as he was ready to help, he recoiled from meddling. To meddle is to destroy the holy chance. Meddlesomeness is the very opposite of helpfulness, for it consists in forcing your self into another self, instead of opening your self as a refuge to the other.

Paul Faber, Surgeon

INDEPENDENCE

[The laird] was more and more for himself, and thereby losing his life. Dearly as he loved his daughter, he was, by slow fallings away, growing ever less of a companion, less of a comfort, less of a necessity to her, and requiring less and less of her for the good or ease of his existence. We wrong those near us in being independent of them. God himself would not be happy without his Son. We ought to lean on each other, giving and receiving — not as weaklings, but as lovers. Love is strength as well as need.

The Elect Lady

Alas for Scotland that such families are now to seek! Would that the parliaments of our country held such a proportion of noble-minded men as was once to be found in the clay huts on a hillside, or grouped about a central farm, huts whose wretched look would move the pity of many a man as inferior to their occupants as a King Charles's lap-dog is to a shepherd's collie. The utensils of their life were mean enough: the life itself was often *elixir vitae* — a true family life, looking up to the high, divine life. But well for the world that such a life has been scattered over it, east and west, the seed of fresh growth in new lands. Out of offence to the individual, God brings good to the whole; for he pets no nation, but trains it for the perfect globular life of all nations — of his world — of his universe. As he makes families mingle, to redeem each from its family selfishness, so will he make nations mingle, and love and correct and reform and develop each other, till the planet world shall go singing through space one harmony to the God of the whole earth. The excellence must vanish from one portion, that it may be diffused through the whole. The seed ripens on one favoured mound, and is scattered over the plain. We console ourselves with the higher thought, that if Scotland is worse, the world is better.

Robert Falconer

It is not house, and fire, and plenty of servants, and all the things that money can procure, that make a home — not father or mother or friends; but one heart which will not be weary of helping, will not be offended with the petulance of sickness, nor the ministrations needful to weakness: this 'entire affection hating nicer hands' will make a home of a cave in a rock, or a gipsy's tent.

David Elginbrod

Orba thought: John was always reasonable, and that is more than can be said of most men. Some, indeed, who are reasonable enough with men, are often unreasonable with women. If in course of time the management of affairs be taken from men and given to women — which may God for our sakes forbid — it will be because men have made it necessary by their arrogance. But when they have been kept down long enough to learn that they are not the lords of creation one bit more than the weakest woman, I hope they will be allowed to take the lead again, lest women should become what men were, and go strutting in their importance.

The Flight of the Shadow

And here I may remark in regard to one of the vexed questions of the day — the rights of women — that what women demand it is not for men to withhold. It is not their business to lay down the law for women. That women must lay down for themselves. I confess that, although I must herein seem to many of my readers old-fashioned and conservative, I should not like to see any woman I cared for either in parliament, or in an anatomical class-room; but on the other hand I feel that women must be left free to settle that matter. If it is not good, good women will find it out and recoil from it. If it is good, then God give them good speed.

The Seaboard Parish

All, *from the cope*
Of heaven down to my windows, in a cone
Still widening upward, mine! for my love born!
Saint-sisters, hero-brothers, known, unknown,
Beloved faces, many as ears of corn
Bending one way on autumn harvest-field,
Leaned downwards to my windowed hut forlorn,
As if with power of eyes they would have healed
The heart that lay there moaning selfish fears.
Faces that with one look might each have sealed
For evermore one fount of bitter tears!
Each face a lamp of God, from which did pass
The light of worship out on all its peers!
Each knowing self only in others' glass;
Seeking no love, or worship, or other grace,
Which ever endeth in a deep alas,
But offering evermore the heart-embrace!
Each form upheld in crowding arms of love,
Each heart upholding all the human race!
A cloud of chosen witnesses above,
Came narrowing thus to me in mystic cone.

Poetical Works

Some as they approach middle age, some only when they are old, wake up to understand that they have parents. To some the perception comes with their children; to others with the pang of seeing them walk away light-hearted out into the world, as they themselves turned their backs on their parents: they had been all their own, and now they have done with them! Less or more have we not all thus taken our journey into a far country? But many a man of sixty is more of a son to the father gone from the earth, than he was while under his roof. What a disintegrated mass were the world, what a lump of half-baked brick, if death were indeed the end of affection! if there were no chance more of setting right what was so wrong in the loveliest relations! How gladly would many a son who once thought it a weariness to serve his parents, minister now to their lightest need! and in the boundless eternity is there no help?

Home Again

But [Malcolm] had now arrived at that season when, in the order of things, a man is compelled to have at least a glimmer of the life which consists in sharing life with another. When once, through the thousand unknown paths of creation, the human being is so far divided from God that his individuality is secured, it has become yet more needful that the crust gathered around him in the process should be broken; and the love between man and woman, arising from a difference deep in the heart of God, and essential to the very being of each — for by no words can I express my scorn of the evil fancy that the distinction between them is solely or even primarily physical — is one of his most powerful forces for blasting the wall of separation, and, first step towards the universal harmony, of twain making one.

Malcolm

He who by a mother's love
Made the wandering world his own,
Every year comes from above,
Binding Earth to the Father's throne.

Nay, thou comest every day!
No, thou never didst depart!
Never hour hast been away!
Always with us, Lord, thou art,
Binding, binding heart to heart!

Poetical Works

It seems to me, also, that in thinking of the miseries and wretchedness in the world we too seldom think of the other side. We hear of an event in association with some certain individual, and we say — 'How dreadful! How miserable!' And perhaps we say — 'Is there — can there be a God in the earth when such a thing can take place?' But we do not see into the region of actual suffering or conflict. We do not see the heart where the shock falls. We neither see the proud bracing of energies to meet the ruin that threatens, nor the gracious faint in which the weak escape from writhing. We do not see the abatement of pain which is paradise to the tortured; we do not see the gentle upholding in sorrow that comes even from the ministrations of nature — not to speak of human nature — to delicate souls. In a word, we do not see, and the sufferer himself does not understand, how God is present every moment, comforting, upholding, heeding that the pain shall not be more than can be borne, making the thing possible and not hideous.

Guild Court

When Rogers had thanked God, he rose, took my hand, and said:—

'Mr Walton, you *will* preach now. I thank God for the good we shall all get from the trouble you have gone through.'

'I ought to be the better for it,' I answered.

'You *will* be the better for it,' he returned. 'I believe I've allus been the better for any trouble as ever I had to go through with. I couldn't quite say the same for every bit of good luck I had; leastways, I consider trouble the best luck a man can have. And I wish you a good night, sir. Thank God! again.'

'But, Rogers, you don't mean it would be good for us to have bad luck always, do you? You shouldn't be pleased at what's come to me now, in that case.'

'No, sir, sartinly not.'

'How can you say, then, that bad luck is the best luck?'

'I mean the bad luck that comes to us — not the bad luck that doesn't come. But you're right, sir. Good luck or back luck's both best when *He* sends 'em, as he allus does. In fac', sir, there is no bad luck but what comes out o' the man hisself. The rest's all good.'

Annals of a Quiet Neighbourhood

No troubles are for one moment to be compared with those that come of the wrongness, even if it be not wickedness, that is our own. Some clouds rise from stagnant bogs and fens; others from the wide, clean, large ocean. But either kind, thank God, will serve the angels to come down by. In the old stories of celestial visitants the clouds do much; and it is oftenest of all down the misty slopes of griefs and pains and fears, that the most powerful joy slides into the hearts of men and women and children.

Mary Marston

God loves not sorrow, yet rejoices to see a man sorrowful, for in his sorrow man leaves his heavenward door on the latch, and God can enter to help him. He loves, I say, to see him sorrowful, for then he can come near to part him from that which makes his sorrow a welcome sight.

The Hope of the Gospel

[Cosmo] saw for the first time clearly how the Jews came to assign evil to the hand of God as well as good, and what St Paul meant when he said that the law gave life to sin; for by the sun is the shadow; where no light is there is no darkness, where no life, no death. He saw too that in the spiritual world what we need is a live sun strong enough to burn up all the shadows by shining through the things that cast them, and compelling their transparency — and that the sun is the God who is light and in whom is no darkness at all — which truth is the gospel according to St John. And where there is no longer anything covered or hid, shall sin be able to live? Can it go on without dens and caves and shadows?

Castle Warlock

The best thing that can happen to a man, sometimes, is to lose his money; and while people are compassionate over the loss, God may regard it as the first step of the stair by which the man shall rise above it and many other things besides with which not only his feet, but his hands and head are defiled.

Guild Court

[Cosmo's father] knew what the sharp things of life are to the human plant; that its frosts are needful as well as its sunshine, its great passion-winds as well as its gentle rains; that an imperative result is required, that his human son had to be made divine, and that in aid of this end man must humbly follow the great lines of Nature, ready to withhold his hand, anxious not to interfere. Many would foil the marvellous process, call in worldly wisdom to guide to other and worldly ends, bring the experience of their own failures to bear for the production of worse. But he who would escape the mill that grinds slow and small, must yield to the hammer and chisel; for those who refuse to be stones of the living temple must be ground into mortar for it.

Castle Warlock

Now wicked fairies will not be bound by the laws which the good fairies obey, and this always seems to give the bad the advantage over the good, for they use means to gain their ends which the others will not. But it is all of no consequence, for what they do never succeeds; nay, in the end it brings about the very thing they are trying to prevent. So you see that, somehow, for all their cleverness, wicked fairies are dreadfully stupid, for, although from the beginning of the world they have really helped instead of thwarting the good fairies, not one of them is a bit the wiser for it. She will try the bad thing just as they all did before her; and succeed no better of course.

At the Back of the North Wind

HAPPY PILGRIMS

Does not the Bible itself tell us that we are pilgrims and strangers in the world, that here we have no abiding city? It is but a place to which we come to be made ready for another. Yet I am sure that those who regard is as their home, are not half so well pleased with it as I. They are always grumbling at it. 'What wretched weather!' they say. 'What a cursed misfortune!' they cry. 'What abominable luck!' they protest. Health is the first thing, they say, and cannot find it. They complain that their plans are thwarted, and when they succeed, that they did not yield the satisfaction they expected. Yet they mock at him who says he seeks a better country!

What's Mine's Mine

But why should it be possible to mistrust —
Nor possible only, but its opposite hard?
Why should no man believe because he must —
By sight's compulsion? Why should he be scarred
With conflict? worn with doubting fine and long? —
No man is fit for heaven's musician throng
Who has not tuned an instrument all shook and
    jarred.

Diary of an Old Soul

157
TRUE POSSESSION

Which is the real possessor of a book — the man who has its original and every following edition, and shows, to many an admiring and envious visitor, now this, now that, in binding characteristic with possession-pride; yea, from secret shrine is able to draw forth and display the author's manuscript, with the very shapes in which his thoughts came forth to the light of day — or the man who cherishes one little, hollow-backed, coverless, untitled, bethumbed copy, which he takes with him in his solitary walks and broods over in his silent chamber, always finding in it some beauty or excellence or aid he had not found before — which is to him in truth as a live companion? . . . Just so may the world itself be possessed . . . as a book filled with words from the mouth of God, or but as the golden-clasped covers of that book; as an embodiment or incarnation of God himself; or but as a house built to sell.

The Hope of the Gospel

158
A GOOD FALL

It is the kindest thing God can do for his children sometimes, to let them fall in the mire. You would not hold by your Father's hand; you struggled to pull it away; he let it go, and there you lay. Now that you stretch forth the hand to him again, he will take you, and clean, not your garments only, but your heart, and soul, and consciousness.

Guild Court

CHEERFULNESS

I found cheerfulness to be like life itself — not to be created by any argument. Afterwards I learned, that the best way to manage some kinds of painful thoughts, is to dare them to do their worst; to let them lie and gnaw at your heart till they are tired; and you find you still have a residue of life they cannot kill.

Phantastes

KINDNESS FROM FAITH

It was Friday night, and Diamond, like the rest of the household, had had very little to eat that day. The mother would always pay the week's rent before she laid out anything even on food. His father had been very gloomy — so gloomy that he had actually been cross to his wife. It is a strange thing how the pain of seeing the suffering of those we love will sometimes make us add to their sufferings by being cross with them. This comes of not having faith enough in God, and shows how necessary this faith is, for when we lose it, we lose even the kindness which alone can soothe the suffering.

At the Back of the North Wind

TO FIND GOD

I *would go near thee — but I cannot press*
Into thy presence — it helps not to presume.
Thy doors are deeds; the handles are their doing.
He whose day-life is obedient righteousness,
Who, after failure, or a poor success,
Rises up, stronger effort yet renewing —
He finds thee, Lord, at length, in his own common
  room.

Diary of an Old Soul

BEYOND FEELINGS

Feelings are not scientific instruments for that which surrounds them; they but speak of themselves when they say, 'I am cold; I am dark.' The final perfection will be when our faith is utterly and absolutely independent of our feelings. I dare to imagine such the final victory of our Lord — when he followed the cry of 'Why hast thou forsaken me?' with — 'Father, into thy hands I commend my spirit.'

Castle Warlock

JOY AND SORROW

As in all sweetest music, a tinge of sadness was in every note. Nor do we know how much of the pleasures even of life we owe to the intermingled sorrows. Joy cannot unfold the deepest truths, although deepest truth must be deepest joy.

Phantastes

THE SUFFERINGS OF JESUS

It is with the holiest fear that we should approach the terrible fact of the sufferings of our Lord. Let no one think that those were less because he was more. The more delicate the nature, the more alive to all that is lovely and true, lawful and right, the more does it feel the antagonism of pain, the inroad of death upon life; the most dreadful is that breach of the harmony of things whose sound is torture.

Unspoken Sermons

Things come to the poor that can't get in at the door of the rich. Their money somehow blocks it up. It is a great privilege to be poor, Peter — one that no man ever coveted, and but a very few have sought to retain, but one that yet many have learned to prize. You must not mistake, however, and imagine it as a virtue; it is but a privilege, and one also that, like other privileges, may be terribly misused.

The Princess and Curdie

But whether Poppie, when speaking the worst language that ever crossed her lips, was lower, morally and spiritually considered, than the young lord in the nursery, who, speaking with articulation clear-cut as his features, and in language every word of which is to be found in Johnson, refuses his brother a share of his tart and gobbles it up himself, there is to me, knowing that if Poppie could swear she could share, no question whatever. God looks after his children in the cellars as well as in the nurseries of London.

Guild Court

I CAN'T HELP IT

Cosmo was not one of those poor creatures who, finding in themselves certain tendencies with whose existence they had nothing to do, therefore in whose presence they have no blame, will say to themselves, 'I cannot help it,' and at once create evil, and make it their own, by obeying the inborn impulse. Inheritors of a lovely estate, with a dragon in a den which they have to kill that the brood may perish, they make friends with the dragon, and so think to save themselves trouble!

Castle Warlock

RIPENESS

This weariness of mine, may it not come
From something that doth need no setting right?
Shall fruit be blamed if it hang wearily
A day before it perfected drop plumb
To the sad earth from off its nursing tree?
Ripeness must always come with loss of might,
The weary evening fall before the resting night.

Diary of an Old Soul

THE OUTWARD WORLD

This outward world is but a passing vision of the persistent true. We shall not live in it always. We are dwellers in a divine universe where no desires are in vain, if only they be large enough. Not even in this world do all disappointments breed only vain regrets.

A Dish of Orts

170

GOD GIVES

*To give a thing and take again
Is counted meanness among men;
Still less to take what once is given
Can be the royal way of heaven!*

*But human hearts are crumbly stuff,
And never, never love enough;
And so God takes and, with a smile,
Puts our best things away awhile.*

*Some therefore weep, some rave, some scorn;
Some wish they never had been born;
Some humble grow at last and still,
And then God gives them what they will.*

Poetical Works

OBSTRUCTIONS

Our Lord never mentions poverty as one of the obstructions to his kingdom, neither has it ever proved such; riches, cares, and desires he does mention.

Weighed and Wanting

MERCIFUL EARTHQUAKES

James said, 'Some people nothing but an earthquake will rouse from their dead sleep: I was one of such. God in his mercy brought on the earthquake: it woke me and saved me from death. Ignorant creatures go about asking why God permits evil: we know why! It may be He could with a word cause evil to cease — but would that be to create good? The word might make us good like oxen or harmless sheep, but would that be a goodness worthy of him who was made in the image of God? If a man ceased to be *capable* of evil, he must cease to be a man! . . . For the sake of this, that we may come to choose the good, all the discipline of the world exists.

Salted with Fire

But must we believe that Judas, who repented even to agony, who repented so that his high-prized life, self, soul became worthless in his eyes and met with no mercy at his own hand — must we believe that he could find no mercy in such a God ? I think, when Judas fled from his hanged and fallen body, he fled to the tender help of Jesus, and found it — I say not how. He was in a more hopeful condition now than during any moment of his past life, for he had never repented before. But I believe that Jesus loved Judas even when he was kissing him with the traitor's kiss; and I believe that he was his Saviour still.

Unspoken Sermons

There are tender-hearted people who virtually object to the whole scheme of creation; they would neither have force used not pain suffered; they talk as if kindness could do everything, even where it is not felt. Millions of human beings but for suffering would never develop an atom of affection. The man who would spare due suffering is not wise. It is folly to conclude a thing ought not to be done because it hurts. There are powers to be born, creations to be perfected, sinners to be redeemed, through the ministry of pain, that could be born, perfected, redeemed in no other way.

What's Mine's Mine

175

A BETTER WAY

Better to love than be beloved,
Though lonely all the day;
Better the fountain in the heart,
Than the fountain by the way.

Better than thrill a listening crowd,
Sit at a wise man's feet;
But better teach a child, than toil
To make thyself complete.

Better a death when work is done,
Than earth's most favoured birth;
Better a child in God's great house,
Than the King of all the earth.

Poetical Works

176

SOLITUDE

It was a poor hut, mostly built of turf; but turf makes warm walls, impervious to the wind, and it was a place of her own! — that is, she had it to herself, a luxury many cannot even imagine, while to others to be able to be alone at will seems one of the original necessities of life. Even the Lord, who probably had not always a room to himself in the poor houses he staid at, could not do without solitude; therefore not unfrequently spent the night in the open air, on the quiet, star-served hill: there even for him it would seem to have been easier to find an entrance into that deeper solitude which, it is true, he did not need in order to come into closer contact with him who was the one joy of his life, whether his hard life on earth or his blessed life in heaven.

What's Mine's Mine

It is like the Father, too, not to withhold good wine because men abuse it. Enforced virtue is unworthy of the name. That men may rise above temptation it is needful that they should have temptation. It is the will of him who makes the grapes and the wine. Men will even call Jesus himself a wine-bibber. What matter it, so long as he works as the Father works, and lives as the Father wills?

The Miracles of Our Lord

178

DISSATISFACTION

Dissatisfaction is but the reverse of the medal of life. So long as a man is satisfied, he seeks nothing; when a fresh gulf is opened in his being, he must rise and find wherewithal to fill it. Our history is the opening of such gulfs, and the search for what will fill them.

There and Back

As he refused to make stones bread, so throughout [his] life he never wrought a miracle to help himself; as he refused to cast himself from the temple to convince Satan or glory visibly in his Sonship, so he steadily refused to give the sign which the human Satans demanded, notwithstanding the offer of conviction which they held forth to bribe him to the grant. How easy it seems to have confounded them, and strengthened his followers! But such a conviction would stand in the way of a better conviction in his disciples, and would do his adversaries only harm. For neither could not in any true sense be convinced by such a show: it could but prove his power. It might prove so far the presence of a God, but would it prove that God? Would it bring him nearer to them who could not see him in the face of his Son? To say *'Thou art God'* without knowing what the Thou means — of what use is it? God is a name only, except we know *God*. Our Lord did not care to be so acknowledged.

Unspoken Sermons

Surely if a man would help his fellow-men, he can do so far more effectively by exhibiting truth than by exposing error, by unveiling beauty than by a critical dissection of deformity. From the very nature of the thing it must be so. Let the true and good destroy their opposites. It is only by the good and beautiful that the evil and ugly are known.

A Dish of Orts

There are thousands for whom a blow is a better thing than expostulation, persuasion, or any sort of kindness. They are such that nothing but a blow will set their door ajar for love to get in. That is why hardships, troubles, disappointments, and all kinds of pain and suffering, are sent to so many of us. We are so full of ourselves, and feel so grand, that we should never come to know what poor creatures we are, never begin to do better, but for the knock-down blows that the living God gives us. We do not like them, but he does not spare us for that.

A Rough Shaking

TRUE FREEDOM

So bound in selfishness am I, so chained,
I know it must be glorious to be free,
But know not what, full-fraught, the word doth
  mean.
By loss on loss I have severely gained
Wisdom enough my slavery to see;
But liberty, pure, absolute, serene,
No freest-visioned slave has ever seen.

Diary of an Old Soul

183
GOD'S UNFINISHED WORK

[Richard said] 'If you're right, miss, and there be a God, either he's not so good as you would be if you were God, or else somebody interferes, and won't let him do his best.'

'Shall I tell you what [Mr Wingfold] said the other day?' returned Barbara. 'He said that it was not fair, when a man had made something for a purpose, to try to say it was not good before we knew what his purpose with it was. "I don't like", he said, "even my wife to look at my verses before they're finished! God can't hide away his work till it is finished, as I do my verses, and we ought to take care what we say about it. God wants to do something better with people than people think."'

There and Back

NO FORCE

All good news from heaven is of *truth* — essential truth, involving duty, and giving and promising help to the performance of it. There can be no good news for us men, except of uplifting love, and no one can be lifted up who will not rise. If God himself sought to raise his little ones without their consenting effort, they would drop from his foiled endeavour. He will carry us in his arms till we are able to walk; he will carry us in his arms when we are weary with walking; he will not carry us if we will not walk.

The Hope of the Gospel

Perhaps the highest moral height which a man can reach, and at the same time the most difficult of achievement, is the willingness to be *nothing* relatively, so that he attain that positive excellence which the original conditions of his being render not merely possible, but imperative . . . God makes the glow-worm as well as the stars; the light in both is divine. If mine be an earth star to gladden the wayside, I must cultivate humbly and rejoicingly its green earth-glow, and not seek to blanch it to the whiteness of the stars that lie in the fields of blue. For to deny God in my own being is to cease to behold him in any. God and man can meet only by the man's becoming that which God meant him to be. Then he enters into the house of life, which is greater than the house of fame. It is better to be a child in a green field than a knight of many orders in a state ceremonial.

A Dish of Orts

There are two sins, not of individual deed, but of spiritual condition, which *cannot be forgiven*; that is, as it seems to me, which cannot be excused, passed by, made little of by the tenderness even of God, inasmuch as they will allow no forgiveness to come into the soul, they will permit no good influence to go on working alongside of them; they shut God out altogether. Therefore the man guilty of these can never receive into himself the holy renewing saving influences of God's forgiveness. God is outside of him in every sense, save that which springs from his creating relation to him, by which, thanks be to God, he yet keeps a hold of him, although against the will of the man who will not be forgiven. The one of these sins is against man; the other against God. The former is unforgiveness to our neighbour; the shutting him out from our mercies, from our love — so from the universe, as far as we are a portion of it — the murdering therefore of our neighbour. It may be an infinitely less evil to murder a man than to refuse to forgive him. The former may be the act of a moment of passion: the latter is the heart's choice. It is *spiritual* murder, the worst, to hate, to brood over the feeling that excludes, that kills the image, the idea of the hated.

Unspoken Sermons

EVENING HYMN

O God, whose daylight leadeth down
Into the sunless way,
Who with restoring sleep dost crown
The labour of the day!

What I have done, Lord, make it clean
With thy forgiveness dear;
That so to-day what might have been,
To-morrow may appear.

Poetical Works

188

APOSTOLIC DARING

Imagine St Paul having a prevision of how he would be misunderstood, *and heeding it!* — what would then have become of all his most magnificent outbursts? And would any amount of apostolic carefulness have protected him? I suspect it would only have given rise to more vulgar misunderstandings and misrepresentations still. To explain to him that loves not, is but to give him the more plentiful material for misinterpretation.

Thomas Wingfold, Curate

GROWTH IN CHRIST

The sole way to put light into the wing,
To preen its feathers, and to make them grow,
Is to heed humbly even the smallest thing
With which the Christ in us has aught to do.
So will that Christ from child to manhood go,
Obedient to the father Christ; and so
Sweet holy change will turn all our old things to new.

Diary of an Old Soul

THE SHADOW LOST

Then first I knew the delight of being lowly; of saying to myself, 'I am what I am, nothing more.' 'I have failed,' I said; 'I have lost myself — would it had been my shadow.' I looked round: the shadow was nowhere to be seen. Ere long I learned that it was not myself, but only my shadow, that I had lost. I learned that it is better, a thousand-fold, for a proud man to fall and be humbled, than to hold up his head in his pride and fancied innocence. I learned that he that will be a hero, will barely be a man; that he that will be nothing but a doer of his work, is sure of his manhood. In nothing was my ideal lowered, or dimmed, or grown less precious; I only saw it too plainly, to set myself for a moment beside it. Indeed, my ideal soon became my life; whereas, formerly, my life had consisted in a vain attempt to behold, if not my ideal in myself, at least myself in my ideal. Now, however, I took, at first, what perhaps was a mistaken pleasure, in despising and degrading myself. Another self seemed to arise, like a white spirit from a dead man, from the dumb and trampled self of the past. Doubtless, this self must again die and be buried, and again, from its tomb, spring a winged child; but of this my history bears not as yet the record. Self will come to life even in the slaying of self; but there is ever something deeper and stronger than it, which will emerge at last from the unknown abysses of the soul: will it be as a solemn gloom, burning with eyes? or a clear morning after the rain? or a smiling child, that finds itself nowhere, and everywhere?

Phantastes

191
CAPABLE OF MURDER

There was a time when I could not understand that he who loved not his brother was a murderer: now I see it to be no figure of speech, but, in the realities of man's moral and spiritual nature, an absolute simple fact. The murderer and the unloving sit on the same bench before the judge of eternal truth. The man who loves not his brother, I do not say is at this moment capable of killing him, but if the natural working of his unlove be not checked, he will assuredly become capable of killing him.

Thomas Wingfold, Curate

DON'T EXCUSE : CONFESS

I wonder how it would be with souls if they waked up and found all their sins but hideous dreams! How many would loathe the sin? How many would remain capable of doing all again? But few, perhaps no burdened souls can have any idea of the power that lies in God's forgiveness to relieve their consciousness of defilement. Those who say, 'Even God cannot destroy the fact!' care more about their own cursed shame than their Father's blessed truth! Such will rather excuse than confess. When a man heartily confesses, leaving excuses to God, the truth makes him free, he knows that the evil has gone from him, as a man knows that he is cured of his plague.

Donal Grant

193
HEART-OPEN-HOUSE

I do not fear the greatness of thy command —
To keep heart-open-house to brother men;
But till in thy God's love perfect I stand,
My door not wide enough will open. Then
Each man will be love — awful in my sight;
And open to the eternal morning's might,
Each human face will shine my window for thy
light.

Diary of an Old Soul

But here there is no room for ambition. Ambition is the desire to be above one's neighbour; and here there is no possibility of comparison with one's neighbour: no one knows what the white stone contains except the man who receives it. Here is room for endless aspiration towards the unseen ideal; none for ambition. Ambition would only be higher than others; aspiration would be high. Relative worth is not only unknown — to the children of the kingdom it is unknowable. Each esteems the other better than himself. How shall the rose, the glowing heart of the summer heats, rejoice against the snowdrop risen with hanging head from the white bosom of the snow? Both are God's thoughts; both are dear to him; both are needful to the completeness of his earth and the revelation of himself.

Unspoken Sermons

NO COMPARISON

It is nothing to a man to be greater or less than another; to be esteemed or otherwise by the public or private world in which he moves. Does he, or does he not, behold and love and live the unchangeable, the essential, the divine? This he can only do according as God has made him. He can behold and understand God in the least degree as well as in the greatest, only by the godlike within him; and he that loves thus the good and great has no room, no thought, no necessity for comparison and difference. The truth satisfies him, He lives in its absoluteness.

Adela Cathcart

RAG-RIGHTS

Lord, I have fallen again — a human clod!
Selfish I was, and heedless to offend;
Stood on my rights. Thy own child who would not
   send
Away his shreds of nothing for the whole God!
Wretched, to thee who savest, low I bend:
Give me the power to let my rag-rights go
In the great wind that from thy gulf doth blow.

Diary of an Old Soul

He was evidently at strife with himself: he knew he was wrong, but could not yet bring himself to say so. It is one of the poorest of human weaknesses that a man should be ashamed of saying he has done wrong, instead of so ashamed of having done wrong that he cannot rest till he has said so; for the shame cleaves fast until the confession removes it.

Donal Grant

198
CONTEMPT

Contempt is murder committed by the intellect, as hatred is murder committed by the heart. Charity having life in itself, is the opposite and destroyer of contempt as well as of hatred.

David Elginbrod

What a hell of horror, I thought, to wander alone, a bare existence never going out of itself, never widening its life in another life, but, bound with the cords of its poor peculiarities, lying an eternal prisoner in the dungeon of its own being! I began to learn that it was impossible to live for oneself even, save in the presence of others — then, alas, fearfully possible! evil was only through good! selfishness but a parasite on the tree of life! In my own world I had the habit of solitary song; here not a crooning murmur passed my lips! There I sang without thinking; here I thought without singing! there I had never had a bosom-friend; here the affection of an idiot would be divinely welcome! 'If only I had a dog to love!' I sighed — and regarded with wonder my past self, which preferred the company of book or pen to that of man or woman; which, if the author of a tale I was enjoying appeared, would wish him away that I might return to his story. I had chosen the dead rather than the living, the thing thought rather than the thing thinking! 'Any man,' I said now, 'is more than the greatest of books!' I had not cared for my live brothers and sisters, and now I was left without even the dead to comfort me.

Lilith

GROWING

There are two ways of growing. You may be growing up, or you may be growing down; and if you are doing both at once, then you are growing crooked. There are people who are growing up in understanding, but down in goodness. It is a beautiful fact, however, that you can't grow up in goodness and down in understanding; while the great probability is, that, if you are not growing better, you will by and by grow stupid. Those who are growing the right way, the more they understand, the more they wonder; and the more they learn to do, the more they want to do.

Gutta Percha Willie

NO STRANGE PLACE

No place on earth henceforth I shall count strange,
For every place belongeth to my Christ.
I will go calm where'er thou bid'st me range;
Whoe'er my neighbour, thou art still my nighest.

Diary of an Old Soul

POSSESSION

Things go wrong, generally, because men have such absurd and impossible notions about *possession*. They call things their own which it is impossible, from their very nature, ever to possess or make their own. Power was never given to man over men for his own sake, and the nearer he that so uses it comes to success, the more utter will prove his discomfiture.

Donal Grant

DOWNRIGHT FORGIVENESS

Make my forgiveness downright — such as I
Should perish if I did not have from thee;
I let the wrong go, withered up and dry,
Cursed with divine forgetfulness in me.
'Tis but self-pity, pleasant, mean, and sly,
Low whispering bids the paltry memory live:—
What am I brother for, but to forgive!

Diary of an Old Soul

AN UNWORTHY GOD

People that only care to be saved, that is, not to be punished for their sins, are anxious only about themselves, not about God and his glory at all. They talk about the glory of God, but they make it consist in pure selfishness! According to them, he seeks everything for himself; which is dead against the truth of God, a diabolic slander of God. It does not trouble them to believe such things about God; they do not even desire that God should not be like that; they only want to escape him.

The Elect Lady

MAN'S WRATH

Keep me from wrath, let it seem ever so right:
My wrath will never work thy righteousness.
Up, up the hill, to the whiter than snow-shine,
Help me to climb, and dwell in pardon's light.
I must be pure as thou, or ever less
Than thy design of me — therefore incline
My heart to take men's wrongs as thou tak'st mine.

Diary of an Old Soul

LEVELLING UP

When I see a man lifting up those that are beneath him, not pulling down those that are above him, I will believe in his communism. Those who most resent being looked down upon, are in general the readiest to look down upon others. It is not principle, it is not truth, it is themselves they regard. Of all false divinities, Self is the most illogical.

The Elect Lady

POSTERITY

[Mary Magdalene's] is a curious instance of the worthlessness of what some think it a mark of high-mindedness to regard alone — the opinion, namely, of posterity. Without a fragment of evidence, this woman has been all but universally regarded as impure. But what a trifle to her! Down in this squabbling nursery of the race, the name of Mary Magdalene may be degraded even to a subject for pictorial sentimentalities; but the woman herself is with that Jesus who set her free. To the end of time they may call her what they please: to her it is worth but a smile of holy amusement. And just as worthy is the applause of posterity associated with a name. To God alone we live or die. Let us fall, as, thank him, we must, into his hands. Let him judge us. Posterity may be wiser than we; but posterity is not our judge.

The Miracles of Our Lord

208

PATIENT DILIGENCE

Make me all patience and all diligence;
Patience, that thou may'st have thy time with me;
Diligence, that I waste not thy expense
In sending out to bring me home to thee.
What though thy work in me transcends my sense —
Too fine, too high, for me to understand —
I hope entirely. On, Lord, with thy labour grand.

Diary of an Old Soul

Not one of them being capable of enjoying anything by herself, together they were unable to enjoy much; and, like the miser, who, when he cannot much enjoy his money, desires more, began to desire more company to share in the already withering satisfaction of their new possession — to help them, that is, to get pleasure out of it, as out of a new dress. It is a good thing to desire to share a good thing, but it is not well to be unable alone to enjoy a good thing. It is our enjoyment that should make us desirous to share. What is there to share if the thing be of no value in itself? To enjoy alone is to be able to share. No participation can make that of value which in itself is of none. It is not love alone but pride also, and often only pride, that leads to the desire for another to be present with us in possession.

What's Mine's Mine

POWER

Power that is not of God, however great,
Is but the downward rushing and the glare
Of a swift meteor that hath lost its share
In the one impulse which doth animate
The parent mass: emblem to me of fate!
Which through vast nightly wastes doth onward fare,
Wild-eyed and headlong, rent away from prayer —
A moment brilliant, then most desolate!
And O my brother, shall we ever learn
From all the things we see continually
That pride is but the empty mockery
Of what is strong in man. Not so the stern
And sweet repose of soul which we can earn
Only through reverence and humility.

Poetical Works

ROUGH-HEWN GOODNESS

Remember, Lord, thou hast not made me good
Or if thou didst, it was so long ago
I have forgotten — and never understood,
I humbly think.
At best it was a crude,
A rough-hewn goodness, that did need this woe,
This sin, these harms of all kinds fierce and rude,
To shape it out, making it live and grow.

Diary of an Old Soul

THE WIDOW'S MITE

Cast in your coins, for God delights
When from wide hands they fall;
But here is one who brings two mites,
And thus gives more than all.

I think she did not hear the praise —
Went home content with need;
Walked in her poor generous ways,
Nor knew her heavenly meed.

Poetical Works

BLACK AND WHITE

Christina was of that numerous class of readers, who, if you show one thing better than another, will without hesitation report that you love the one and hate the other. If you say, for instance, that it is a worse and yet more shameful thing for a man to break his wife's heart by systematic neglect, than to strike her and be sorry for it, such readers give out that you approve of wife-beating, and perhaps write to you to expostulate with you on your brutality. If you express pleasure that a poor maniac should have succeeded in escaping through the door of death from his haunting demon, they accuse of you of advocating suicide.

What's Mine's Mine

SELF-EXAMINATION

I suspect that self-examination is seldom the most profitable, certainly it is sometimes the most unpleasant, and always the most difficult of moral actions — that is, to perform after a genuine fashion. I know that very little of what passes for it has the remotest claim to reality; and I will not say that it has never to be done; but I am certain that a good deal of the energy spent by some devout and upright people on trying to understand themselves and their own motives, would be expended to better purpose and with far fuller attainment even in regard to that object itself, in the endeavour to understand God, and what he would have us to do.

The Marquis of Lossie

LIVE TRULY

Our business is not to think correctly, but to live truly; then first will there be a possibility of our thinking correctly. One chief cause of the amount of unbelief in the world is, that those who have seen something of the glory of Christ, set themselves to theorize concerning him rather than to obey him. In teaching men, they have not taught them Christ, but taught them about Christ.

Unspoken Sermons

As to his higher nature, the farmer believed in God — that is he tried to do what God required of him, and thus was on the straight road to know him. He talked little about religion, and was no partisan. When he heard people advocating or opposing the claims of this or that party in the church, he would turn away with a smile such as men yield to the talk of children. He had no time, he would say, to spend on such disputes: he had enough to do trying to practise what was beyond dispute.

Salted with Fire

217
DOING, NOT UNDERSTANDING

The greatest obscuration of the words of the Lord, as of all true teachers, comes from those who give themselves to interpret rather than do them. Theologians have done more to hide the gospel of Christ than any of its adversaries. It was not for our understandings, but our will, that Christ came. He who does that which he sees, shall understand; he who is set upon understanding rather than doing, shall go on stumbling and mistaking and speaking foolishness.

The Miracles of Our Lord

TWO THINGS AT ONCE

Two things at once, thou know'st I cannot think,
When busy with the work thou givest me,
I cannot consciously then think of thee.
Then why, when next thou lookest o'er the brink
Of my horizon, should my spirit shrink,
Reproached and fearful, nor to greet thee run?
Can I be two when I am only one?

Diary of an Old Soul

219

WORK

Labour is not in itself an evil like the sickness, but often a divine, a blissful remedy. Nor is the duty or the advantage confined to those who ought to labour for their own support. No amount of wealth sets one free from the obligation to work — in a world the God of which is ever working. He who works not has not yet discovered what God made him for, and is a false note in the orchestra of the universe. The possession of wealth is as it were a pre-payment, and involves an obligation of honour to the doing of correspondent work. He who does not know what to do has never seriously asked himself what he ought to do.

The Miracles of Our Lord

Though the Bible contains many an utterance of the will of God, we do not need to go there to find how to begin to do his will. In every heart there is a consciousness of some duty or other required of it: that is the will of God. He who would be saved must get up and do that will — if it be but to sweep a room or make an apology, or pay a debt. It was he who had kept the commandments whom Jesus invited to be his follower in poverty and labour.

from a letter

'When you have a thing to do,' Andrew would say, 'you will do it right in proportion to your love of right. But do the right, and you will love the right; for by doing it you will see it in a measure as it is, and no one can see the truth as it is without loving it. The more you *talk* about what is right, or even about the doing of it, the more you are in danger of exemplifying how loosely theory may be allied to practice. Talk without action saps the very will. Something you have to do is waiting undone all the time, and getting more and more undone. The only refuge is *to do*.'

The Elect Lady

THE TRUE KINGDOM

What is the true life of a nation? That, I answer, which favours the growth within the individual of that kingdom of heaven for the sake only of which the kingdoms of earth exist. The true life of the people, as distinguished from the nation, is simply the growth of its individuals in those eternal principles of truth, in proportion to whose power in them they take rank in the kingdom of heaven, the only kingdom that can endure, all others being but as the mimicries of children playing at government.

England's Antiphon

223
NO BURDEN

I cannot see, my God, a reason why
From morn to night I go not gladsome, free;
For, if thou art what my soul thinketh thee,
There is no burden but should lightly lie,
No duty but a joy at heart must be.

Diary of an Old Soul

IGNORE THE DEVIL

[Donal said] 'He who does what the devil would have him do, is the man who believes in him, not he who does not care whether he is or not, so long as he avoids doing his works. If there be such a one, his last thought must be to persuade men of his existence! He is a subject I do not care to discuss; he is not very interesting to me.'

Donal Grant

THE RICH YOUNG MAN

[The rich young man] would doubtless have gladly devoted his wealth to the service of the master, yea and gone with him, *as a rich man*, to spend it for him. But part with it to free him for his service — that he could not — *yet*! . . . Why should he not keep it? Why not use it in the service of the Master? What wisdom could there be in throwing away such a grand advantage? He could devote it, but he could not cast it from him! He could devote it, but he could not devote himself! . . . How could a rich man believe he would be of more value without his money? . . . Had he done as the Master told him, he would soon have come to understand. Obedience is the opener of eyes.

Unspoken Sermons

HARD WORK

I believe not a few keep hold of their senses in virtue of doing hard work. I knew an earl's son and heir who did so. And I think that not a few, especially women, lose their senses just from having nothing to do. Many more, who are not in danger of this, lose their health, and more still lose their purity and rectitude. In other words, health — physical, mental, moral, and spiritual — requires for its existence and continuance, work, often hard and bodily labour.

Guild Court

NOT WHAT WE CHOOSE

'It is so easy,' continued Donal, 'to do the thing we ordain ourselves, for in holding to it we make ourselves out fine fellows ! — and that is such a mean kind of thing ! Then when another who has the right, lays a thing upon us, we grumble — though it be the truest and kindest thing, and the most reasonable and needful for us — even for our dignity — for our being worth anything ! Depend upon it, Davie, to do what we are told is a far grander thing than to lay the severest rules upon ourselves — ay, and to stick to them, too !'

Donal Grant

LAW AND WILL

The kingdom of heaven is not come, even when God's will is our law: it is come when God's will is our will. While God's will is our law, we are but a kind of noble slaves; when his will is our will, we are free children.

David Elginbrod

OBEDIENCE

The story of Christ and the appeals of those who had handled the Word of Life had another end in view than making people understand how God arranged matters to save them. God would have us live; if we live we cannot but know; all the knowledge in the universe could not make us live. Obedience is the road to all things — the only way in which to grow able to trust him. Love and faith and obedience are sides of the same prism.

Donal Grant

※

[The rich young man] wanted eternal life: to love God with all his heart, and soul, and strength, and mind, is to know God, and to know him *is* eternal life; that is the end of the whole saving matter; it is no human beginning, it is the grand and eternal beginning of all things; but the youth was not capable of it. To begin with that would be as sensible as to say to one asking how to reach the top of some mountain, 'Just set your foot on that shining snow-clad peak, high there in the blue, and you will at once be where you wish to go.' 'Love God with all your heart, and eternal life is yours' — it would have been to mock him . . . The Lord answers his question directly, tells him what to do — a thing he can do — to enter into life: he must keep the commandments! — and when he asks, 'Which?' specifies only those that have to do with his neighbour, ending with the highest and most difficult of them.

Unspoken Sermons

PROGRESS BY OBEDIENCE

[Mary] was as yet, in relation to the gospel, such as the Jews were in relation to their law: they had not yet learned the gospel of their law, and she was yet only serving the law of the gospel. But she was making progress, in simple and pure virtue of her obedience. Show me the person ready to step from any, let it be the narrowest sect of Christian Pharisees into a freer and holier air, and I shall look to find in that person the one of that sect who, in the midst of its darkness and selfish worldliness, mistaken for holiness, has been living a life more obedient than the rest.

Mary Marston

IF THE LORD CAME TODAY

If the Lord were to appear this day in England as once in Palestine, he would not come in the halo of the painters, or with that wintry shine of effeminate beauty, or sweet weakness, in which it is their helpless custom to represent him. Neither would he probably come as a carpenter, or mason, or gardener. He would come in such form and condition as might bear to the present England, Scotland, and Ireland, a relation like that which the form and condition he then came in, bore to the motley Judea, Samaria, and Galilee . . .

One thing is certain: they who first recognized him would be those that most loved righteousness and hated iniquity.

Unspoken Sermons

233
THE FIRST STEP

[Willie] had long ago seen that those who are doomed not to realize their ideal, are just those who will not take the first step towards it. 'Oh! this is such a little thing to do, it can't be any use!' they say. 'And it's such a distance off what I mean, and what I should give my life to have!' They think and they say that they would give their life for it, and yet they will not give a single hearty effort. Hence they just stop where they are, or rather go back and back until they do not care a bit for the thoughts they used to think so great that they cherished them for the glory of having thought them. But even the wretched people who set their hearts on making money, begin by saving the first penny they can, and then the next and the next. And they have their reward: they get the riches they want — with the loss of their souls to be sure, but that they did not think of. The people on the other hand who want to be noble and good, begin by taking the first thing that comes to their hand and doing that right, and so they go from one thing to another, growing better and better.

Gutta Percha Willie

LIVE

My own conviction is, that if a man would but bend his energies to *live*, if he would but try to be a true, that is, a godlike man, in all his dealings with his fellows, a genuine neighbour and not a selfish unit, he would open such channels for the flow of the spirit as no amount of even honest and so-called successful preaching could.

Malcolm

235
DIVINE DISCONTENT

Discontent is the life in us that has not enough of itself, is not enough to itself, so calls for more. He has the victory who, in the midst of pain and weariness, cries out, not for death, not for the repose of forgetfulness, but for strength to fight; for more power, more consciousness of being, more God in him; who, when sorest wounded, says with Sir Andrew Barton in the old ballad:

> *Fight on my men, Sir Andrew said,*
> *I am but hurt, but I am not slain;*
> *I'll lay me down and bleed awhile,*
> *And then I'll rise and fight again;*

— and that with no silly notion of playing the hero —
what have creatures like us to do with heroism who
are not yet barely honest! — but because so to fight is
the truth, and the only way.

Unspoken Sermons

236

THE SWEEPER OF THE FLOOR

Methought that in a solemn church I stood.
Its marble acres, worn with knees and feet,
Lay spread from door to door, from street to street.
Midway the form hung high upon the rood
Of Him who gave His life to be our good;
Beyond priests flitted, bowed, and murmured meet,
Among the candles shining still and sweet.
Men came and went, and worshipped as they could...
And still their dust a woman with her broom
Bowed to her work, kept sweeping to the door.
Then saw I, slow through all the pillared gloom,
Across the church, a silent figure come:
'Daughter,' it said, 'thou sweepest well My floor!'
'It is the Lord!' I cried, and saw no more.

Poetical Works

237
DUTY

When a man's duty looks like an enemy, dragging him into the dark mountains, he has no less to go with it than when, like a friend with loving face, it offers to lead him along green pastures by the river side.

Annals of a Quiet Neighbourhood

238
NO EFFORT

She sometimes wished she were good; but there are thousands of wandering ghosts who would be good if they might without taking trouble: the kind of goodness they desire would not be worth a life to hold it.

What's Mine's Mine

'But no man can perfectly keep a single command-ment of the second table any more than of the first.'

Surely not — else why should they have been given? But is there no meaning in the word *keep*, or *observe*, except it be qualified by *perfectly*? Is there no keeping but a perfect keeping?

'None that God cares for.'

There I think you utterly wrong. That no keeping but a perfect one will satisfy God, I hold with all my heart and strength; but that there is none else he cares for, is one of the lies of the enemy. What father is not pleased with the first tottering attempts of his little one to walk? What father would be satisfied with anything but the manly step of the full-grown son?

Unspoken Sermons

To try too hard to make people good, is the one way to make them worse; that the only way to make them good is to be good — remembering well the beam and the mote; that the time for speaking comes rarely, the time for being never departs.

Sir Gibbie

WORK

Those who think it hard to have to work hard as well as endure other sore trials, little know how much those other trials are rendered endurable by the work which accompanies them. They regard the work as an additional burden, instead of as the prop which keeps their burdens from crushing them to the earth. The same is true of pain — sometimes of grief, sometimes of fear.

Donal Grant

ONLY INDIVIDUALS SIN

The philanthropist who regards the wrong as in the race, forgetting that the race is made up of conscious and wrong individuals, forgets also that wrong is always generated in and done by an individual; that the wrongness exists in the individual, and by him is passed over, as tendency, to the race; and that no evil can be cured in the race, except by its being cured in its individuals: tendency is not absolute evil; it is there that it may be resisted, not yielded to. There is no way of making three men right but by making right each one of the three; but a cure in one man who repents and turns, is a beginning of the cure of the whole human race.

The Hope of the Gospel

Malcolm was one of the few who understand the shelter of light, the protection to be gained against lying tongues by the discarding of needless reticence, and the open presentation of the truth. Many men who would not tell a lie, yet seem to have faith in concealment: they would rather not reveal the truth; darkness seems to offer them the cover of a friendly wing. But there is no veil like light — no adamantine armour against hurt like the truth. To Malcolm it was one of the promises of the kingdom that there is nothing covered that shall not be revealed.

The Marquis of Lossie

Do those who say, lo here and lo there are the signs of his coming, think to be too keen for him, and spy his approach? When he tells them to watch lest he find them neglecting their work, they stare this way and that, and watch lest he should succeed in coming like a thief! So throughout: if instead of speculation, we gave ourselves to obedience, what a difference would soon be seen in the world! Oh, the multitude of so-called religious questions which the Lord would answer with, 'Strive to enter in at the strait gate!' Many eat and drink and talk and teach in his presence; few do the things he says to them! Obedience is the one key of life.

Unspoken Sermons

DIVINE PATIENCE

'Of one thing I am pretty sure,' Falconer resumed, 'that the same recipe Goethe gave for the enjoyment of life, applies equally to all work : "Do the thing that lies next to you." That is all our business. Hurried results are worse than none. We must force nothing, but be partakers of the divine patience. How long it took to make the cradle ! and we fret that the baby Humanity is not reading Euclid and Plato, even that it is not understanding the Gospel of St John ! If there is one thing evident in the world's history, it is that God hasteneth not. All haste implies weakness. Time is as cheap as space and matter. What they call the church militant is only at drill yet, and a good many of the officers too not out of the awkward squad !'

Robert Falconer

TRUE WORTH

Peter's delight was in the open air, and hard work in it. He was as far from the vulgar idea that a man rose in the scale of honour when he ceased to labour with his hands, as he was from the fancy that a man rose in the kingdom of heaven when he was made a bishop.

Salted with Fire

To let their light shine, not to force on them their interpretation of God's designs, is the duty of Christians towards their fellows. If you who set yourselves to explain the theory of Christianity, had set yourselves instead to do the will of the Master, the one object for which the Gospel was preached to you, how different would now be the condition of that portion of the world with which you come into contact! Had you given yourselves to the understanding of his word that you might do it, and not to the quarrying from it of material wherewith to buttress your systems, in many a heart by this time would the name of the Lord be loved where now it remains unknown. The word of life would then by you have been held out indeed.

Unspoken Sermons

THE ANCHOR OF THE SOUL

He had ever one anchor of the soul, and he found that it held — the faith of Jesus (I say the faith of Jesus, not his own faith in Jesus), the truth of Jesus, the life of Jesus. However his intellect might be tossed on the waves of speculation and criticism, he found that the word the Lord had spoken remained; for in doing righteously, in loving mercy, in walking humbly, the conviction increased that Jesus knew the very secret of human life.

Robert Falconer

249

LOVE FOR ALL

I well remember feeling as a child that I did not care for God to love me if he did not love everybody: the kind of love I needed was the love that all men needed, the love that belonged to their nature as the children of the father, a love he could not give me except he gave it to all men.

Weighed and Wanting

I overheard a part of what the cottager was saying, and could not help listening to the rest,

'And the man was telling them, sir, that God had picked out so many men, women, and children, to go right away to glory, and left the rest to be damned for ever and ever in hell. And I up and spoke to him; and "Sir," says I, "if I was tould as how I was to pick out so many out o' my childeren, and take 'em with me to a fine house, and leave the rest to be burnt up i' the old one, which o' them would I choose?" "How can I tell?" says he. "No doubt," says I; "they aint your sons and darters. But I can. I wouldn't move a foot, sir, but I'd take my chance wi' the poor things. And, sir" says I, "we're all God's childeren; and which o' us is he to choose, and which is he to leave out? I don't believe he'd know a bit better how to choose one and leave another than I should, sir — that is, his heart wouldn't let him lose e'er a one o' us, or he'd be miserable for ever, as I should be, if I left one o' mine i' the fire."'

Adela Cathcart

[Robert said] 'Weel, gin I win in there [Heaven], the verra first nicht I sit doon wi' the lave o' them, I'm gain' to rise up an' say — that is, gin the maister, at the heid o' the table, disna bid me sit doon — an' say: "Brithers an' sisters, the haill o' ye, hearken to me for ae minute; an', O Lord! gin I say wrang, jist take the speech frae me, and I'll sit doon dumb an' rebukit. We're a' here by grace and no by merit, save his, as ye a' ken better nor I can tell ye, for ye hae been langer here nor me. But it's jist ruggin' an' rivin' at my hert to think o' them 'at's doon there. Maybe ye can hear them. I canna. Noo, we hae nae merit, an' they hae nae merit, an' what for are we here and them there? But we're washed clean and innocent noo; and noon, whan there's no wyte lying upo' oorsel's, it seems to me that we micht beir some o' the sins o' them 'at hae ower mony. I call upo' ilk o' ye 'at has a frien' or a neebor doon yonder, to rise up an' taste nor bite nor sup mair till we gang up a' thegither to the fut o' the throne, and pray the Lord to lat's gang and du as the maister did afor's, and beir their griefs, and cairry their sorrows doon in hell there; gin it may be that they may repent and get remission o' their sins, an' come up here wi' us at the lang last, and sit doon wi' 's at this table, a' throuw the merits o' oor Saviour Jesus Christ, at the heid o' the table there. Amen."'

Robert Falconer

'What is the priest,' thought Mr Fuller. 'Just a man to be among men what the Sunday is among the work days of the week — a man to remind you that there is a life within this life, or beyond and about it, if you like that mode better — for extremes meet in the truest figures — that care is not of God, that faith and confidence are truer, simpler, more of common sense than balances at bankers or preference shares. He is a protest against the money-heaping tendencies of men, against the desire of rank or estimation or any kind of social distinction. With him all men are equal, as in the Church all have equal rights, and rank ceases on the threshold of the same, overpowered by the presence of the Son of Mary, who was married to a carpenter.'

Guild Court

I will not attempt an account of the sermon; even admirably rendered, it would be worthless as the best of copies of a bad wall-paper. There was in it, to be sure, such a glowing description of the city of God as might have served to attract thither all the diamond-merchants of Amsterdam; but why a Christian should care to go to such a place, let him tell who knows; while, on the other hand, the audience appeared equally interested in his equiponderating description of the place of misery. Not once did he attempt to give, or indeed could have given, the feeblest idea, to a single soul present, of the one terror of the universe — the peril of being cast from the arms of essential Love and Life into the bosom of living Death. For this teacher of men knew nothing whatever but by hearsay, had not in himself experienced one of the joys or one of the horrors he endeavoured to embody.

Sir Gibbie

How terribly, then, have the theologians misrepresented God! Nearly all of them represent him as a great King on a grand throne, thinking how grand he is, and making it the business of his being and the end of his universe to keep up his glory, wielding the bolts of a Jupiter against them that take his name in vain. They would not allow this, but follow out what they say, and it comes much to this.

Brothers, have you found our king? There he is, kissing little children and saying they are like God. There he is at table with the head of a fisherman lying on his bosom, and somewhat heavy at heart that even he, the beloved disciple, cannot yet understand him well. The simplest peasant who loves his children and his sheep were — no, not a truer, for the other is false, but — a true type of our God beside that monstrosity of a monarch.

Unspoken Sermons

It is God we want, not heaven; his righteousness, not an imputed one, for our own possession; remission, not letting off; love, not endurance for the sake of another, even if that other be the one loveliest of all.

Donal Grant

One grand aim of the reformers of the Scottish ecclesiastical modes, appears to have been to keep the worship pure and the worshippers sincere, by embodying the whole in the ugliest forms that could be associated with the name of Christianity. It might be wished, however, that some of their followers, and amongst them the clergyman of the church in question, had been content to stop there; and had left the object of worship, as represented by them, in the possession of some loveable attribute; so as not to require a man to love that which is unloveable, or worship that which is not honourable — in a word, to bow down before that which is not divine. The cause of this degeneracy they share in common with the followers of all other great men as well as of Calvin. They take up what their leader, urged by the necessity of the time, spoke loudest, never heeding what he loved most; and then work the former out to a logical perdition of everything belonging to the latter.

David Elginbrod

[The minister] was a man of not merely dry or stale, but of deadly doctrines. He would have a man love Christ for protecting him from God, not for leading him to God in whom alone is bliss, out of whom all is darkness and misery. He had not a glimmer of the truth that eternal life is to know God. He imagined justice and love dwelling in eternal opposition in the bosom of eternal unity.

He knew next to nothing about God, and misrepresented him hideously. If God were such as he showed him, it would be the worst possible misfortune to have been created.

Donal Grant

I know another clergyman — perhaps my readers may know him too — who instead of lecturing Thomas through the medium of a long string of scriptural phrases, which he would have had far too much reverence to use after such a fashion, would have taken him by the shoulder, and said, 'Tom, my boy, you've got something on your mind. I hope it's nothing wrong. But whatever it is, mind you come to me if I can be of any use to you.'

Guild Court

Coming home with a great, grand fox-glove in his hand, [Cupples] met some of the missionars returning from their chapel, and amongst the rest Robert Bruce, who stopped and spoke.

'I'm surprised to see ye carryin' that thing o' the Lord's day, Mr Cupples. Fowk'll think ill o' ye.'

'Weel, ye see, Mr Bruce, it angert me sae to see the ill-faured thing positeevly growin' there upo' the Lord's day, that I pu'd it up 'maist by the reet. To think o' a weyd like that prankin' itsel' oot in its purple and its spots upo' the Sawbath day! It canna ken what it's aboot. I'm only feared I left eneugh o' 't to be up again afore lang.'

Alec Forbes of Howglen

MORAL POLICEMEN

The way the legally righteous act the policeman in the moral world would be amusing were it not so sad. They are always making the evil 'move on', driving it to do its mischiefs to other people instead of them; dispersing nests of the degraded to crowd them the more, and with worse results, in other parts: why should such be shocked at the idea of sending out of the world those to whom they will not give a place in it to lay their heads? They treat them in this world as, according to the old theology, their God treats them in the next, keeping them alive for sin and suffering.

Donal Grant

261
THE MINISTER THE MAN

Some clergymen separate themselves and their office to a degree which I cannot understand. To assert the dignities of my office seems to me very like exalting myself; and when I have had a twinge of conscience about it, as has happened more than once, I have then found comfort in these two texts: 'The Son of Man came not to be ministered unto but to minister;' and 'It is enough that the servant should be as his master.' Neither have I ever been able to see the very great difference between right and wrong in a clergyman, and right and wrong in another man. All that I can pretend to have discovered comes to this : that what is right in another man is right in a clergyman ; and what is wrong in another man is much worse in a clergyman.

Annals of a Quiet Neighbourhood

THE NEED TO THINK

[Andrew said] 'Let nane o' the lovers o' law an' letter perswaud ye the Lord wadna hae ye think — though nane but him 'at obeys can think wi' safety. We maun do first the thing 'at we ken, an' syne we may think aboot the thing 'at we dinna ken. I fancy 'at whiles the Lord wadna say a thing jist no to stop fowk thinkin' aboot it. He was aye at gettin' them to make use o' the can'le o' the Lord. It's my belief the main obstacles to the growth o' the kingdom are first the oonbelief o' believers, an' syne the w'y 'at they lay doon the law. Afore they hae learnt the rudimen's o' the trowth themsel's, they begin to lay the grievous burden o' their dullness an' ill-conceived notions o' holy things upo' the min's an' consciences o' their neebours, fain, ye wad think, to haud them frae growin' only mair nor themsel's.

Donal Grant

GOD AND THE OLD TESTAMENT

Like many other children far more carefully taught of man, she was labouring under the misery of the fancy that everything related in the Old Testament without remark of disapprobation is sanctioned by the divine will. If parents do not encourage their children to speak their minds about what they read generally, and especially in the Bible, they will one day be dismayed to find that they have not merely the strangest but the most deadly notions of what is contained in that book — as, for instance, that God approved of all the sly tricks of Jacob — for was not he the religious one of the brothers, and did not all his tricks succeed? They are not able without help to regard the history broadly, and see that just because of this bad that was in him, he had to pass through a life of varied and severe suffering, punished in the vices which his children inherited from himself, in order that the noble part of his nature might be burned clean of the filth that clung to it.

Guild Court

OUTWARD FORMS

I remember also he said, that those, however good they might be, who urged attention to the forms of religion, such as going to church and saying prayers, were, however innocently, just the prophets of

Pharisaism; that what man had to be stirred up to was to lay hold upon God, and then they would not fail to find out what religious forms they ought to cherish.

The Vicar's Daughter

NO CONDESCENSION

'Did you hear Mr Rackstraw's sermon on the condescension of God?' asked Alexa.

'The condescension of God, ma'am! There is no such thing. God never condescended with one Jove-like nod, all his mighty, eternal life! God condescend to his children — their spirits born of his spirit, their hearts the children of his heart! No, ma'am! there never was a falser, uglier word in any lying sermon!'

His eyes flashed and his face shone. Alexa thought she had never seen him look so grand.

'I see,' she answered. 'I will never use the word about God again!'

'Thank you, ma'am.'

'Why should you thank me?'

'I beg your pardon; I had no right to thank you. But I am so tried with the wicked things said about God by people who think they are speaking to his pleasure and not in his despite, that I am apt to talk foolishly. I don't wonder at God's patience with the wicked, but I do wonder at his patience with the pious!'

The Elect Lady

SECTARIANISM

I doubt if wickedness does half as much harm as sectarianism, whether it be the sectarianism of the church or of dissent, the sectarianism whose virtue is condescension, or the sectarianism whose vice is pride. Division has done more to hide Christ from the view of men, than all the infidelity that has ever been spoken. It is the half-Christian clergy of every denomination that are the main cause of the so-called failure of the church of Christ. Thank God, it has not failed so miserably as to succeed in the estimation or to the satisfaction of any party in it.

Paul Faber, Surgeon

THE BIBLE AND JESUS

The one use of the Bible is to make us look at Jesus, that through him we may know his Father, his God, and our God. Till we thus know him let us hold the Bible dear as the moon of our darkness, by which we travel towards the east; not dear as the sun whence her light cometh, and towards which we haste, that, walking in the sun himself, we may no more need the mirror that reflects his absent brightness.

Unspoken Sermons

By cam a minister o' the kirk:
'A sair mishanter!' he cried;
'Wha kens whaur the villains may lirk!
I's haud to the ither side!'

By cam an elder o' the kirk;
Like a young horse he shied:
'Fie! here's a bonnie mornin's wark!'
An' he spangt to the ither side.

By cam ane gaed to the wrang kirk;
Douce he trottit alang.
'Puir body!' he cried, an' wi' a yerk
Aff o' his cuddy he sprang.

He ran to the body, an' turnt it ower:
'There's life i' the man!' he cried.
He wasna ane to stan' an' glower,
Nor haud to the ither side!

Poetical Works

For [the dull disciple] all revelation has ceased and been buried in the Bible, to be with difficulty ex-humed and, with much questioning of the decayed form, re-united into a rigid skeleton of metaphysical and legal contrivance . . . Sad indeed would the whole matter be, if the Bible had told us *everything* God meant us to believe. But herein is the Bible itself greatly wronged. It nowhere lays claim to be regarded as *the* Word, *the* Way, *the* Truth. The Bible leads us to Jesus, the inexhaustible, the ever unfolding Revela-tion of God. It is Christ ' in whom are hid all the treasures of wisdom and knowledge,' not the Bible, save as leading to him. And why are we told that these treasures are *hid* in him who is the *Revelation* of God ? Is it that we should despair of finding them and cease to seek them ? Are they not hid in him that they may be revealed to us in due time — that is, when we are in need of them ? . . . to say that we must wait for the other world, to know the mind of him who came to this world to give himself to us, seems to me the foolishness of a worldly and lazy spirit.

Unspoken Sermons

I think I have learned since, that the parson of a parish must be content to keep the upper windows of his mind open to the holy winds and the pure light of heaven; and the side windows of tone, of speech, of behaviour open to the earth, to let forth upon his fellow-men the tenderness and truth which those upper influences bring forth in any region exposed to their operation. Believing in his Master, such a servant shall not make haste; shall feel no feverous desire to behold the work of his hands; shall be content to be as his Master, who waiteth long for the fruits of His earth.

Annals of a Quiet Neighbourhood

And then [Wingfold] began to discover one peculiar advantage belonging to the little open chamber of the pulpit — open not only or specially to heaven above, but to so many of the secret chambers of the souls of the congregation. For what a man dares not, could not if he dared, and dared not if he could, say to another, even at the time and in the place fittest of all, he can say thence, open-faced before the whole congregation; and the person in need thereof may hear it without umbrage, or the choking husk of individual application, irritating to the rejection of what truth may lie in it for him.

Thomas Wingfold, Curate

'We dinna hear 'at the Saviour himsel' ever sae much as smiled,' said Thomas.

Annie answered: 'Weel, that wad hae been little wonner, wi' what he had upo' 'm. But I'm nae sure that he didna, for a' that. Fowk disna aye tell when a body lauchs. I'm thinkin' gin ane o' the bairnies that he took upo' 's knee, — an' he was ill-pleased wi' them 'at wad hae sheued them awa', — gin ane o' them had hauden up his wee timmer horsie, wi' a broken leg, and had prayed him to work a miracle an' men' the leg, he wadna hae wrocht a miracle maybe, I daursay, but he wad hae smilet, or maybe lauchen a wee, and he wad hae men't the leg some gait or ither to please the bairnie. And gin't had been me, I wad raither hae had the men'in o' 's ain twa han's, wi' a knife to help them maybe, nor twenty miracles upon' 't.'

Alec Forbes of Howglen

TRUE GOD

Surely the only refuge from heathenish representations of God under Christian forms, the only refuge from man's blinding and paralysing theories, from the dead wooden shapes substituted for the living forms of human love and hope and aspiration, from the interpretations which render scripture as dry as a speech in Chancery — surely the one refuge from these awful evils is the Son of man; for no misrepresentation and no misconception can destroy the beauty of that face which the marring of sorrow has elevated into the region of reality, beyond the marring of irreverent speculation and scholastic definition. From the God of man's painting, we turn to the man of God's being, and he leads us to the true God, the radiation of whose glory we first see in him.

David Elginbrod

They dare not say God will not do this or that, however clear it be that it would not be fair; they are in terror of contradicting the Bible. They make more of the Bible than of God, and so fail to find the truth of the Bible, and accept things concerning God which are not in the Bible, and are the greatest of insults to him! . . . The God that many people believe in, claiming to be *the* religious because they believe in him, is a God not worth believing in, a God that ought not to be believed in.

The Elect Lady

275

THE CLERGYMAN

If the clergyman cannot rouse men to seek his God and their God, if he can only rest in his office, which becomes false the moment he rests in it, being itself for a higher end; if he has no message from the infinite to quicken the thoughts that cleave to the dust, the sooner he takes to grave-digging or any other honest labour, the sooner will he get into the kingdom of heaven, and the higher he will stand in it.

Guild Court

[St Paul] knew nothing of the so-called Christian systems that change the glory of the perfect God into the likeness of the low intellects and dull consciences of men — a worse corruption than the representing of him in human shape. What kind of soul is it that would not choose the Apollo of light, the high-walking Hyperion, to the notion of the dull, self-cherishing monarch, the law-dispensing magistrate, or the cruel martinet, generated in the pagan arrogance of Rome, and accepted by the world in the church as the portrait of its God! Jesus Christ is the *only* likeness of the living Father.

Unspoken Sermons

The good mother was not, however, one of those conceited, stiff-necked, power-loving souls who have been the curse and ruin of the church in all ages; she was but one of those in whom reverence for its passing form dulls the perception of unchangeable truth. They shut up God's precious light in the horn lantern of human theory, and the lantern casts such shadows on the path of the kingdom as seem to dim eyes insurmountable obstructions. For the sake of what they count revealed, they refuse all further revelation, and what satisfies them is merest famine to the next generation of the children of the kingdom. Instead of God's truth they offer man's theory, and accuse of rebellion against God such as cannot live on the husks they call food. But ah, home-hungry soul! thy God is not the elder brother of the parable, but the father with the best robe and the ring — a God high above all thy longing, even as the heavens are high above the earth.

What's Mine's Mine

278

GOOD WORKS ?

As to self-righteousness, I think there is far less of that amongst those who regard the works of righteousness as the means of salvation, than amongst those by whom faith itself is degraded into a work of merit — a condition by fulfilling which they become fit for God's mercy; for such is the trick by which the old Adam and the Enemy together are ready enough to play the most orthodox, in despite of the purity of their creed.

Guild Court

PREACHING

[Polwarth said] 'I profess myself a believer in preaching, and consider that in so far as the Church of England has ceased to be a preaching church — and I don't call nine-tenths of what goes by the name of it *preaching* — she has forgotten a mighty part of her high calling. Of course a man to whom no message has been personally given, has no right to take the place of a prophet — and cannot, save by more or less of simulation — but there is room for teachers as well as prophets, and the more need of teachers that the prophets are so few; and a man may right honestly be a clergyman who teaches the people, though he may possess none of the gifts of prophecy.'

Thomas Wingfold, Curate

The Bible is to me the most precious *thing* in the world, because it tells me [Jesus'] story; and what good men thought about him who knew him and accepted him. But the common theory of the inspiration of the words, instead of the breathing of God's truth into the hearts and souls of those who wrote it, and who then did their best with it, is degrading and evil; and they who hold it are in danger of worshipping the letter instead of living in the Spirit, of being idolators of the Bible instead of disciples of Jesus. It is Jesus who is the Revelation of God, not the Bible; that is but a means to a mighty eternal end.

from a letter

281

THE LIFE OF THE CHURCH

The world would not perish if what is called the church did go to pieces; a truer church, for there might well be a truer, would arise out of her ruins. But let no one seek to destroy; let him that builds only take heed that he build with gold and silver and precious stones, not with wood and hay and stubble! If the church were so built, who could harm it! If it were not in part so built, it would be as little worth pulling down as letting stand. There is in it a far deeper and better vitality than its blatant supporters will be able to ruin by their advocacy, or the enviers of its valueless social position by their assaults upon that position.

There and Back

282
PALTRY FAITH

What should I think of my child, if I found that he limited his faith in me and hope from me to the few promises he had heard me utter! The faith that limits itself to the promises of God, seems to me to partake of the paltry character of such a faith in my child — good enough for a Pagan, but for a Christian a miserable and wretched faith.

Unspoken Sermons

283
AMENDMENT

One of the painful things in the dogma of the endless loss of the wicked is that it leaves no room for the righteous to make up to them for the wrong things they did them in this life. For the righteous do the wicked far more wrong than they think — the righteous being all the time, in reality, the wealthy, and the wicked the poor.

Thomas Wingfold, Curate

'I know the man; I know your Mr Wingfold! Since you went, he's been more than once or twice to the smithy to ask after you. He's one o' the right sort, he is! He's a man, he is! — not an old woman in breeches! My Soul! why don't they walk and talk and look like men? Most of 'em as I've seen are no more like men than if they was drawn on the wall with a coal! If they was all like your Mr Wingfold now! Why! the devil wouldn't have a chance! I've a soft heart for the clergy — always had, though every now and then they do turn me sick.'

There and Back

285

ATTITUDES TO JESUS

Homage to will and word of the master, apart from the acceptance of certain doctrines concerning him, was in her eyes not merely defective but dangerous. To love the Lord with the love of truest obedience; to believe him the Son of God and the saver of men with absolute acceptance of the heart was far from enough! it was but sentimental affection!

A certain young preacher in Scotland some years ago, accused by an old lady of preaching works, took refuge in the Lord's sermon on the mount: 'Ow aye!' answered the partisan, 'but he was a varra yoong man whan he preacht that sermon!'

What's Mine's Mine

THE LORD'S SUPPER

'Are we to have the pleasure of your company in our conventicle to-morrow?' he added after a little pause.

'Will ye hae me, Mr Bigg?'

'Most willingly, ma'am: and we'll be still better pleased if you'll sit down with us to the Lord's table afterwards.'

'I gang to the perris-kirk, ye ken,' said Miss Horn, supposing the good man unaware of the fact.

'Oh, I know that, ma'am. But don't you think as we shall, I trust, sit down together to his heavenly supper, it would be a good preparation to sit down together, once at least, to his earthly supper first?'

Malcolm

Happily in those days the platitudes and weary vulgarities of what they call *spiritualism* had not been heard of, at least in those quarters, and the soft light of imagination yet brooded over the wide region of mingled false and true, commonly called Superstition: the most killing poison to the imagination must be a strong course of 'spiritualism'. For myself, I am not so set upon entering the Unknown as to creep through the sewers of it to get in. I would not encounter its lovers of garbage, its thieves, impostors, liars, and canaille of all sorts, except I could serve them. That they are on the other side, that they are what men call dead, is no reason for courting their company, taking them into my confidence, asking their advice. Neither do the cups of luke-warm Bible-and-water, which its apparently respectable inhabitants disperse, arouse in me any thirst.

Castle Warlock

THE LORD OF GLADNESS

The Lord of gladness delights in the laughter of a merry heart. These wedding guests [at Cana] could have done without wine, surely without more wine and better wine. But the Father looks with no esteem upon a bare existence, and is ever working, even by suffering, to render life more rich and plentiful.

The Miracles of Our Lord

289

REAL ASSURANCE

Take it that a vision would make us sure, it follows either that God does not care about the kind of sureness it would give us, or that he does not care for our being made sure in that way. God will have us sure of a thing through knowing its source, the heart whence it comes; that is the only worthy assurance. To know, he will have us go in at the grand entrance of obedient faith. If anyone thinks he has found a back stair, he will find it land him at a doorless wall.

Castle Warlock

CONDENSED GIFTS

The miracles are mightier far than any goings on of nature as beheld by common eyes, dissociating them from a loving Will, but the miracles are surely less than those mighty goings on of nature with God beheld at their heart. In the name of him who delighted to say 'My father is greater than I,' I will say that his miracles in bread and in wine were far less grand and less beautiful than the works of the Father they represented, in making the corn to grow in the valleys, and the grapes to drink the sun-light on the hill-sides of the world, with all their infinitudes of tender gradation and delicate mystery of birth. But the Son of the Father be praised, who, as it were, condensed these mysteries before us, and let us see the precious gifts coming at once from gracious hands — hands that love could kiss and nails could wound.

The Miracles of Our Lord

HIDDEN POWER

'Whate'er he saith unto you, do.'
Out flowed his grapes divine;
Though then, as now, not many knew
Who makes the water wine.

Poetical Works

THE BEST WINE

It is such a thing of course that, when our Lord gave them wine, it would be of the best, that it seems almost absurd to remark upon it. What the Father would make and will make, and that towards which he is ever working, is *the Best*; and when our Lord turns the water into wine it must be very good.

The Miracles of Our Lord

293
MARY'S REQUEST

Poor indeed was the making of the wine in the earthen pots of stone, compared with its making in the lovely growth of the vine with its clusters of swelling grapes — the live roots gathering from the earth the water that had to be borne in pitchers and poured into the great vases; but it is precious as the interpreter of the same, even in its being the outcome of our Lord's sympathy with ordinary human rejoicing. There is however an element in its origin that makes it yet more precious to me — the regard of our Lord to a wish of his mother.

The Miracles of Our Lord

❀

In the transfiguration of Jesus we have, I think, just the perfect outcome of those natural results of which we have the first signs in Moses — the full daylight, of which his shining face was as the dawn. Thus, like the other miracles, I regard it as simply a rare manifestation of the perfect working of Nature. Who knows not that in moments of lofty emotion, in which self is for the time forgotten, the eyes shine, and the face is so transfigured that we are doubtful whether it be not in a degree absolutely luminous! I say once more, in the Lord we find the perfecting of all the dull hints of precious things which common humanity affords to us.

The Miracles of Our Lord

The vision in Patmos proved that although Moses must not see the face of God because of its brightness, a more favoured prophet might have the vision. And Tibbie, who had a share in the privileges of the new covenant, who was not under the law like Moses, but under grace like John, would one day see the veil of her blindness shrivel away from before her deeper eyes, burnt up by the glory of that face of God, which is a consuming fire. I suppose that Tibbie was right in the main. But was it not another kind of brightness, a brightness without effulgence, a brightness grander and more glorious, shining in love and patience, and tenderness and forgiveness and excuse, that Moses was unfit to see, because he was not well able to understand it, until, ages after, he descended from heaven upon the Mount of Transfiguration, and the humble son of God went up from the lower earth to meet him there, and talk to him face to face as a man with his friend.

Alec Forbes of Howglen

MORE THAN ENOUGH

'They have no more wine,' she said.
But they had enough of bread!
And the vessels by the door
Held for thirst a plenteous store:
Yes, enough; but Love divine
Turned the water into wine.

Good is all the feasting then;
Good the merry words of men;
Good the laughter and the smiles;
Good the wine that grief beguiles;
Crowning good, the Word divine
Turning water into wine.

May the Master with you dwell;
Daily work this miracle;
In the things that common grow
Waken up the heavenly show;
Ever at your table dine,
Turning water into wine.

Poetical Works

DIVINE SERVICE

We talk of 'divine service.' It is a miserable name for a great thing. It is not service, properly speaking, at all. When a boy comes to his father and says 'May I do so and so for you?' or, rather, comes and breaks out in some way, showing his love to his father — says, 'May I come and sit beside you? May I have some of your books? May I come and be quiet a little in your room?' what would you think of that boy if he went and said, 'I have been doing my father a service'? So with praying to and thanking God, do you call that serving God?

A Dish of Orts

CHURCH OR SERVICE

Remember, if indeed thou art able to know it, that not in any church is the service done that he requires. He will say to no man, 'You never went to church: depart from me; I do not know you;' but 'Inasmuch as you never helped one of my Father's children, you have done nothing for me.'

Unspoken Sermons

If I love and cannot help, does not my heart move me to ask him to help who loves and can? — him without whom life would be to me nothing, without whom I should neither love nor care to pray! – will he answer, 'Child, do not trouble me; I am already doing all I can'? If such answer came, who that loved would not be content to be nowhere in the matter? But how if the eternal, limitless Love, the unspeakable, self-forgetting God-devotion, which, demanding all, gives all, should say, 'Child, I have been doing all I could; but now you are come, I shall be able to do more! here is a corner for you, my little one: push at this thing to get it out of the way'!

The Miracles of Our Lord

[Polwarth said] 'When I use the phrase *divine service*, I mean nothing whatever belonging to the church, or its observances. I mean by it what it ought to mean — the serving of God — the doing of something for God. Shall I make of the church in my foolish imaginations a temple of idolatrous worship by supposing it is for the sake of supplying some need that God has, or of gratifying some taste in him, that I there listen to his word, say prayers to him, and sing his praises?

. . . Talk not of public worship as divine service; it is a mockery. Search the prophets and you will find the observances, fasts and sacrifices and solemn feasts of the temple by them regarded with loathing and scorn, just because by the people they were regarded as *divine service*.

Thomas Wingfold, Curate

Church or chapel is *not* the place for divine service. It is a place of prayer, a place of praise, a place to feed upon good things, a place to learn of God, as what place is not? It is a place to look in the eyes of your neighbour, and love God along with him. But the world in which you move, the place of your living and loving and labour, not the church you go to on your holiday, is the place of divine service. Serve your neighbour and you serve him.

Unspoken Sermons

[Mrs Worboise's] religion was something there, then, not here, now. She would give Mr Simon a five-pound note for his scripture-reading amongst the poor, and the moment after refuse the request of her needlewoman from the same district who begged her to raise her wages from eighteenpence to two shillings a day.

Religion — the bond between man and God — had nothing to do with the earnings of a sister, whose pale face told of 'penury and pine,' a sadder story even than that written upon the countenance of the invalid, for to labour in weakness, longing for rest, is harder than to endure a good deal of pain upon a sofa. Until we begin to learn that the only way to *serve* God in any real sense of the word, is to serve our neighbours, we may have knocked at the wicket-gate, but I doubt if we have got one foot across the threshold of the kingdom.

Guild Court

The last act of our Lord in thus commending his spirit at the close of his life, was only a summing up of what he had been doing all his life. He had been offering this sacrifice, the sacrifice of himself, all the years, and in thus sacrificing he had lived the divine life. Every morning when he went out ere it was day, every evening when he lingered on the night-lapt mountain after his friends were gone, he was offering himself to his Father in the communion of loving words, of high thoughts, of speechless feelings; and, between, he turned to do the same thing in deed, namely, in loving word, in helping thought, in healing action towards his fellows; for the way to worship God while the daylight lasts is to work; the service of God, the only 'divine service,' is the helping of our fellows.

Unspoken Sermons

304

THE PRAYER-BIRD

My prayer-bird was cold — would not away,
Although I set it on the edge of the nest.
Then I bethought me of the story old —
Love-fact or loving fable, thou knowest best —
How, when the children had made sparrows of clay,
Thou mad'st them birds, with wings to flutter and
    fold:
Take, Lord, my prayer in thy hand, and make it
    pray.

Diary of an Old Soul

Jesus *must* have hated anything like display. God's greatest work has never been done in crowds, but in closets; and when it works out from thence, it is not upon crowds, but upon individuals. A crowd is not a divine thing. It is not a body. Its atoms are not members one of another. A crowd is a chaos over which the Spirit of God has yet to move, ere each retires to his place to begin his harmonious work, and unite with all the rest in the organized chorus of the human creation. The crowd must be dispersed that the church may be formed.

The Miracles of Our Lord

306
REAL OFFERING

Mr Walton said, 'God wanted to teach people to offer themselves. Now, you are poor, my pet, and you cannot offer yourself in great things for your fellow-men, which was the way Jesus did. But you must remember that the two young pigeons were just as acceptable to God as the fat bullocks of the rich. Therefore you must say to God something like this:—
'O heavenly Father, I have nothing to offer thee but my patience. I will bear thy will, and so offer my will a burnt-offering unto thee. I will be as useless as thou

pleasest.' Depend upon it, my darling, in the midst of all the science about the world and its ways, and all the ignorance of God and his greatness, the man or woman who can thus say, *Thy will be done*, with the true heart of giving up, is nearer the secret of things than the geologist and theologian.

The Seaboard Parish

WAIT FOR GOD

Everyone that is ready the Father brings to Jesus: the disciple is not greater than his master, and must not think to hasten the hour, or lead one who is not yet taught of God; he must not be miserable about another as if God had forgotten him. Strange helpers of God we shall be, if, thinking to do his work, we act as if he were neglecting it! To wait for God, believing it his one design to redeem his creatures, ready to put his hand to, the minute his hour strikes, is the faith fit for a fellow-worker with him!

Donal Grant

Too eager I must not be to understand.
How should the work the master goes about
Fit the vague sketch my compasses have planned?
I am his house — for him to go in and out.
He builds me now — and if I cannot see
At any time what he is doing with me,
'Tis that he makes the house for me too grand.

The house is not for me — it is for him.
His royal thoughts require many a stair,
Many a tower, many an outlook fair,
Of which I have no thought, and need no care.
Where I am most perplexed, it may be there
Thou mak'st a secret chamber, holy-dim,
Where thou wilt come to help my deepest prayer.

Diary of an Old Soul

'I fancy, perhaps, Mattie, [God] leaves something for us to do. You know they cut out the slop-work at the shop, and I can't do much more with that but put the pieces together. But when a repairing job comes in, I can contrive a bit then, and I like that better.'

Mr Spelt's meaning was not very clear, either to himself or to Mattie. But it involved the shadow of a great truth — that all the discords we hear in the universe around us, are God's trumpets sounding a *reveille* to the sleeping human will, which, once working harmoniously with his, will soon bring all things into a pure and healthy rectitude of operation. Till a man has learned to be happy without the sunshine, and therein becomes capable of enjoying it perfectly, it is well that the shine and the shadow should be mingled, so as God only knows how to mingle them. To effect the blessedness for which God made him, man must become a fellow-worker with God.

Guild Court

Lenorme was silent. He was not altogether innocent of saying prayers; but of late years it had grown a mere formal and gradually a rarer thing. One reason of this was that it had never come into his head that God cared about pictures, or had the slightest interest whether he painted well or ill. If a man's earnest calling, to which of necessity the greater part of his thought is given, is altogether disassociated in his mind from his religion, it is not wonderful that his prayers should by degrees wither and die. The question is whether they ever had much vitality. But one mighty negative was yet true of Lenorme: he had not got in his head, still less had he ever cherished in his heart, the thought that there was anything fine in disbelieving in a God, or anything contemptible in imagining communication with a being of grander essence than himself. That in which Socrates rejoiced with exultant humility, many a youth now-a-days thinks himself a fine fellow for casting from him with ignorant scorn.

The Marquis of Lossie

A MAN'S OWN PLACE IN GOD

There is a chamber also — (O God, humble and accept my speech) — a chamber in God himself, into which none can enter but the one, the individual, the peculiar man — out of which chamber that man has to bring revelation and strength for his brethren. This is that for which he was made — to reveal the secret things of the Father.

Unspoken Sermons

THE PRAYER FOR US

'Help thou mine unbelief.' It is the very triumph of faith. The unbelief itself cast like any other care upon him who careth for us, is the highest exercise of belief. It is the greatest effort lying in the power of the man. No man can help doubt. The true man alone, that is, the faithful man, can appeal to the Truth to enable him to believe what is true, and refuse what is false. How this applies especially to our own time and the need of the living generations, is easy to see. Of all prayers it is the one for us.

The Miracles of Our Lord

HELP GOD WITH PRAYER

Would God give us love, the root of power, in us, and leave that love, whereby he himself creates, altogether helpless in us? May he not at least expedite something for our prayers? Where he could not alter, he could perhaps expedite, in view of some help we might then be able to give. If he desires that we should work with him, that work surely helps him!

Unspoken Sermons

READY FOR THE ASKING

What it would not be well for God to give before a man had asked for it, it may be not only well, but best, to give when he has asked. I believe that the first half of our training is up to the asking point; after that the treatment has a grand new element in it. For God can give when a man is in the fit condition to receive it, what he cannot give before because the man cannot receive it . . . Every parent at all worthy of the relation must know that occasions occur in which the asking of the child makes the giving of the parent the natural correlative. In a way infinitely higher, yet the same at the root, for all is of God, he can give what the man asks what he could not give without, because in the latter case the man would take only the husk of the gift, and cast the kernel away — a husk poisonous without the kernel, although wholesome and comforting with it.

The Miracles of Our Lord

FELLOW-WORKER

Make me a fellow-worker with thee, Christ:
Nought else befits a God-born energy;
Of all that's lovely, only lives the highest,
Lifting the rest that it shall never die.
Up I would be to help thee — for thou liest
Not, linen-swathed in Joseph's garden-tomb,
But walkest crowned, creation's heart and bloom.

Diary of an Old Soul

COOPERATE WITH GOD

The one secret of life and development, is not to devise and plan, but to fall in with the forces at work — to do every moment's duty aright — that being the part in the process allotted to us; and let come — not what will, for there is no such thing — but what the eternal Thought wills for each of us, has intended for each of us from the first. If men would but believe that they are in process of creation, and consent to be made — let the maker handle them as the potter his clay, yielding themselves in respondent motion and submissive hopeful action with the turning of his wheel, they would ere long find themselves able to welcome every pressure of that hand upon them, even when it was felt in pain, and sometimes not only to believe but to recognize the divine end in view, the bringing of a son into glory; whereas, behaving like children who struggle and scream while their mother washes and dresses them, they find they have to be washed and dressed, notwithstanding, and with the more discomfort: they may even have to find themselves set half naked and but half dried in a corner, to come to their right minds, and ask to be finished.

Sir Gibbie

The fact which Lizzie sought to bear upon [Mr Crathie], that our Lord would not have done such a thing, was to him no argument at all. He said to himself, with the superior smile of arrogated commonsense, that 'no mere man since the fall' could be expected to do like him; that he was divine, and had not to fight for a living; that he set us an example that we might see what sinners we were; that religion was one thing, but business was another, and a very proper thing also — with customs and indeed laws of its own far more determinate, at least definite, than those of religion, and that to mingle the one with the other was not merely absurd — it was irreverent and wrong, and certainly never intended in the Bible, which must surely be common sense. It was *the Bible* always with him — never the *will of Christ*.

The Marquis of Lossie

'Jesus buying and selling!' said Wingfold to himself. 'And why not? Did Jesus make chairs and tables, or boats perhaps, which the people of Nazareth wanted, without any admixture of trade in the matter? Was there no transaction? No passing of money between hands? Did they not pay his father for them? Was his Father's way of keeping things going in the world, too vile for the hands of him whose being was delight in the will of that Father? No; there must be a way of handling money that is noble as the handling of the sword in the hands of the patriot. Neither the mean man who loves it, nor the faithless man who despises it, knows how to handle it. The former is one who allows his dog to become a nuisance, the latter one who kicks him from his sight. The noble man is he who so truly does the work given him to do that the inherent nobility of that work is manifest. And the trader who trades nobly is nobler surely than the high-born who, if he carried the principles of his daily life into trade, would be as pitiful a sneak as any that bows and scrapes falsely behind that altar of lies, his counter.'

Thomas Wingfold, Curate

MONEY

Money is not mammon; it is God's invention; it is good and the gift of God. But for money and the need for it, there would not be half the friendship in the world. It is powerful for good when divinely used. Give it plenty of air, and it is sweet as the hawthorn; shut it up, and it cankers and breeds worms. Like all the best gifts of God, like the air and the water, it must have motion and change and shakings asunder; like the earth itself, like the heart and mind of man, it must be broken and turned, not heaped together and neglected.

Paul Faber, Surgeon

AGRIPPA OR PAUL ?

Which is more the possessor of the world — he who has a thousand houses, or he who, without one house to call his own, has ten in which his knock at the door would rouse instant jubilation? Which is the richer — the man who, his large money spent, would have no refuge; or he for whose necessity a hundred would sacrifice comfort? Which of the two possessed the earth — king Agrippa or tent-maker Paul?

The Hope of the Gospel

If the whole power of pedantry should rise against her, the imagination will yet work; and if not for good, then for evil; if not for truth, then for falsehood; if not for life, then for death; the evil alternative becoming the more likely from the unnatural treatment she had experienced from those who ought to have fostered her. The power that might have gone forth in conceiving the noblest forms of action, in realizing the lives of the true-hearted, the self-forgetting, will go forth in building airy castles of vain ambition, of boundless riches, of unearned admiration. The imagination that might be devising how to make the home blessed or to help the poor neighbour, will be absorbed in the invention of the new dress, or worse, in devising the means of procuring it. For, if she be not occupied with the beautiful, she will be occupied by the pleasant; that which goes not out to worship, will remain at home to be sensual. Cultivate the mere intellect as you may, it will never reduce the passions: the imagination, seeking the ideal in everything, will elevate them to their true and noble service.

A Dish of Orts

Few indeed are the Christians capable of understanding [the true relations of money]! The most of them are just where Peter was, when, the moment after the Lord had honoured him as the first to recognize him as the Messiah, he took upon him to object altogether to his master's way of working salvation in the earth. The Roman emperors took up Peter's plan, and the devil has been in the church ever since — Peter's Satan, whom the master told to get behind him. They are poor prophets, and no martyrs, who honour money as an element of any importance in the salvation of the world. Hunger itself does incomparably more to make Christ's kingdom come than ever money did, or ever will do while time lasts. Of course money has its part, for everything has; and whoever has money is bound to use it as best he knows; but his best is generally an attempt to do saint-work by devil-proxy.

Mary Marston

'You can at least tell me what you think of gambling!'

'I think it is the meanest mode of gaining or losing money a man could find.'

'Why do you think so?'

'Because he desires only to gain, and can gain only by his neighbour's loss. One of the two must be the worse for his transaction with the other. Each *must* wish ill to his neighbour!'

'But the risk was agreed between them.'

'True — but in what hope? Was it not, on the part of each, that he would be the gainer and the other the loser? There is no common cause, nothing but pure opposition of interest.'

'Are there not many things in which one must gain and the other lose?'

'There are many things in which one gains and the other loses; but if it is essential to any transaction that only one side shall gain, the thing is not of God.'

The Elect Lady

324
HARD FOR THE RICH

There are many more generous persons among the poor than among the rich — a fact that might help some to understand how a rich man should find it hard to enter into the kingdom of heaven. It is hard for everybody, but harder for the rich. Men who strive to make money are unconsciously pulling instead of pushing at the heavy gate of the kingdom.

A Rough Shaking

MEN OF THE WORLD

Not much passed between them. For one thing the memories of the English lord were not fit to share with the dull old Scotchman beside him who knew nothing of the world. And in truth the laird knew neither how pitilessly selfish, nor how meanly clever, a man of this world may be and bate not a jot of his self-admiration. But men who address a neighbour as a man of the world, paying him the greatest compliment they know in acknowledging him of their kind, recoil with a sort of fear from the man alien to their thoughts, and impracticable for their purposes. They say 'He is beyond me,' and despise him. So is there a world beyond them with which they yet hold a frightful relationship — that of unrecognized, unattempted duty !

Castle Warlock

Now it was clear as day — always provided the man Christ Jesus can be and is with his disciples always to the end of the world — a tradesman might just as soon have Jesus behind the counter with him, teaching him to buy and sell *in his name*, that is as he would have done it, as an earl riding over his lands might have him with him, teaching him how to treat his farmers and cottagers — all depending on how the one did his trading and the other his earling.

Thomas Wingfold, Curate

327
CRIME OR FAULT

[Mary said] 'It doesn't matter whether men call a deed a crime or a fault; the thing is how God regards it, for that is the only truth about it. What the world thinks, goes for nothing, because it is never right. It would be worse in me to do some things the world counts perfectly honourable, than it would be for this man to commit a burglary, or that a murder. I mean my guilt might be greater in committing a respectable sin, than theirs in committing a disreputable one.'

Had Mary know anything of science, she might have said, that, in morals as in chemistry, the qualitative analysis is easy, but the quantitative another affair.

Mary Marston

SOMETHING FOR GOD

I assert that true and genuine service may be rendered to the living God; and, for the development of the divine nature in man, it is necessary that he should do something for God. Nor is it hard to discover how; for God is in every creature that he has made, and in their needs he is needy, and in all their affliction he is afflicted. Therefore Jesus says that whatever is done to one of his little ones is done to him. And if the soul of a man be the temple of the Spirit, then is the place of that man's labour, his shop, his counting-house, his laboratory, the temple of Jesus Christ, where the spirit of man is incarnate in work.

Thomas Wingfold, Curate

329

CHRISTMAS FEASTING

Is it vulgar, this feasting at Christmas? No. It is the Christmas feast that justifies all feasts, as the bread and wine of the Communion are the essence of all bread and wine, of all strength and rejoicing . . . Certain I am, that but for the love which, ever revealing itself, came out brightest at that first Christmas-time, there would be no feasting — nay, no smiling; no world to go careering in joy about its central fire; no men and women upon it, to look up and rejoice.

Adela Cathcart

He was like a seed buried too deep in the soil to which the light has never penetrated, and which, therefore, has never forced its way upwards to the open air, never experienced the resurrection of the dead. But seeds will grow ages after they have fallen into the earth; and, indeed, with many kinds, and within some limits, the older the seed before it germinates, the more plentiful the fruit. And may it not be believed of many human beings, that, the great Husbandman having sown them like seeds in the soil of human affairs, there they lie buried a life long; and only after the upturning of the soil by death, reach a position in which the awakening of their aspiration and the consequent growth become possible. Surely he has made nothing in vain.

Adela Cathcart

331
WHAT SHALL WE BE?

'We ken no more, Maister Sutherlan', what we're growin' till, than that neep-seed there kens what a neep is, though a neep it will be. The only odds is, that we ken that we dinna ken, and the neep-seed kens nothing at all aboot it. But ae thing, Maister Sutherlan', we may be sure o' that whatever it be, it will be worth God's makin' an' our growin'.'

David Elginbrod

'Ah Ruth!' [said Polwarth] 'a bliss beyond speech is waiting for us in the presence of the Master, where, seeing him as he is, we shall grow like him, and be no more either dwarfed or sickly. But you will have the same face, Ruth, else I should be for ever missing something.'

'But you do not think we shall be perfect all at once?'

'No, not all at once; I cannot believe that: God takes time to do what he does — the doing of it is itself good. It would be a sight for heavenly eyes to see you, like a bent and broken and withered lily, straightening and lengthening your stalk, and flushing into beauty. But fancy what it will be to see at length to the very heart of the person you love, and love him perfectly — all that *you* can love *him*! Every love will then be a separate heaven, and all the heavens will blend in one perfect heaven — the love of God — the All in all.'

Paul Faber, Surgeon

'The mair the words o' Jesus come into me,' the doctor began again, 'the surer I am o' seein' my auld Brahmin frien', Robert. It's true I thought his religion not only began but ended inside him. It was a' a booin' doon afore an' an aspirin' up into the bosom o' the infinite God. I dinna mean to say 'at he wasna honourable to them aboot him. And I never saw in him muckle o' that pride to the lave [rest] that belangs to the Brahmin. It was raither a stately kin'ness than that condescension which is the vice o' Christians. But he had naething to do wi' them. The first comman'ment was a' he kent. He loved God — nae a God like Jesus Christ, but the God he kent — and that was a' he could. The second comman'ment — that glorious recognition o' the divine in humanity makin' 't fit an' needfu' to be loved, that claim o' God upon and for his ain bairns, that love o' the neebour as yersel' — he didna ken. Still there was religion in him; and he who died for the sins o' the whole world has surely been revealed to him lang er' noo, and throu the knowledge o' him, he noo dwalls in that God efter whom he aspired.'

Robert Falconer

Art thou not, Jesus, busy like to us?
Thee shall I image as one sitting still,
Ordering all things in thy potent will,
Silent, and thinking ever to thy father,
Whose thought through thee flows multitudinous?
Or shall I think of thee as journeying, rather,
Ceaseless through space, because thou everything
    dost fill?

Diary of an Old Soul

May you have as many happy birthdays in this
world as will make you ready for a happier series of
them afterward, the first of which birthdays will be
the one we call the day of death down here. But there
is a better grander birthday than that which we may
have every day — every hour that we turn away from
ourselves to the living love that makes us love, and so
are born again. And I think all these last birthdays
will be summed up in one transcendent birthday — far
off it may be, but surely to come — the moment when
we know in ourselves that we are one with God, and
are living by his life, and have neither thought or wish
but his.

from a letter

With the sun well risen, I rose, and put my arms as far as they would reach around the beech-tree, and kissed it, and said good-bye. A trembling went through the leaves; a few of the last drops of the night's rain fell from off them at my feet; and as I walked slowly away, I seemed to hear in a whisper once more the words: 'I may love him; for he is a man, and I am only a beech-tree.'

I walked on, in the fresh morning air, as if new-born. The only thing that damped my pleasure was a cloud of something between sorrow and delight, that crossed my mind with the frequently returning thought of my last night's hostess. 'But then,' thought I, 'if she is sorry, I could not help it; and she has all the pleasure she ever had. Such a day as this is surely a joy to her, as much at least as to me. And her life will perhaps be the richer, for holding now within it the memory of what came, but could not stay. And if ever she is a woman, who knows but we may meet somewhere? There is plenty of room for meeting in the universe.'

Phantastes

NO SHADOWY RESURRECTION

Not to believe in mutual recognition beyond, seems to me a far more reprehensible unbelief than that in the resurrection itself. I can well understand how a man should not believe in any life after death. I will confess that although probabilities are for it, *appearances* are against it. But that a man, still more a woman, should believe in the resurrection of the very same body of Jesus, who took pains that his friends should recognize him therein; that they should regard his resurrection as their one ground for the hope of their own uprising, and yet not believe that friend shall embrace friend in the mansions prepared for them, is to me astounding. Such a shadowy resumption of life I should count unworthy of the name of resurrection.

The Miracles of Our Lord

338
WHAT LASTS

His affections, which must live for ever, were set upon that which had passed away. But the child that weeps because his mutilated doll will not rise from the dead, shall yet find relief from his sorrow, a true relief, both human and divine. He shall know that that which in the doll made him love the doll, has not passed away.

Robert Falconer

DEATH WITH GOD

I *was like Peter when he began to sink.*
To thee a new prayer therefore I have got —
That, when Death comes in earnest to my door,
Thou would'st thyself go, when the latch doth clink,
And lead him to my room, up to my cot;
Then hold thy child's hand, hold and leave him not,
Till Death has done with him for evermore.

Diary of an Old Soul

GRAND AND TRUE

'A grand idea,' said Percivale.

'Therefore likely to be a true one,' I returned. 'People find it hard to believe grand things; but why? If there be a God, is it not likely everything is grand, save where the reflection of his great thoughts is shaken, broken, distorted by the watery mirror of our unbelieving and troubled souls? Things ought to be grand, simple, and noble. The ages of eternity will go on showing that such they are and ever have been. God will yet be victorious over our wretched unbeliefs.'

The Seaboard Parish

What boy, however fain to be a disciple of Christ and a child of God, would prefer a sermon to his glorious kite, that divinest of toys, with God himself for his playmate, in the blue wind that tossed it hither and thither in the golden void! He might be ready to part with kite and wind and sun, and go down to the grave for his brothers — but surely not that they might be admitted to an everlasting prayer-meeting! For my own part, I rejoice to think that there will be neither church nor chapel in the high countries; yea, that there will be nothing there called religion, and no law but the perfect law of liberty.

Unspoken Sermons

What a wonderful thing waking is! The time of the ghostly moonshine passes by, and the great positive sunlight comes. A man who dreams, and knows that he is dreaming, thinks he knows what waking is; but knows it so little, that he mistakes, one after another, many a vague and dim change in his dream for an awakening. When the true waking comes at last, he is filled and overflowed with the power of its reality . . . So shall it be with us when we wake from this dream of life into the truer life beyond, and find all our present notions of being, thrown back as into a dim vapoury region of dreamland, where yet we thought we knew, and whence we looked forward into the present. This must be what Novalis means when he says: 'Our life is not a dream; but it may become a dream, and perhaps ought to become one.'

The Portent

NOTHING IS LOST

I think that nothing made is lost,
That not a moon has ever shone,
That not a cloud mine eyes hath crossed,
But to my soul is gone;

That all the lost years garnered lie
In this thy casket, my dim soul;
And thou wilt, once, the key apply,
And show the shining whole.

Poetical Works

A GOOD ATHEIST

It is better to be an atheist who does the will of God, than a so-called Christian who does not. The atheist will not be dismissed because he said *Lord, Lord* and did not obey. The thing that God loves is the only lovely thing, and he who does it, does well, and is upon the way to discover that he does it very badly. When he comes to do it as the will of the perfect Good, then is he on the road to do it perfectly — that is, from love of its own inherent self-constituted goodness, born in the heart of the Perfect. The doing of things from duty is but a stage on the road to the kingdom of truth and love.

Paul Faber, Surgeon

My father was very fond of [his little mare], and used to tell wonderful stories of her judgement and skill. I believe he was never quite without a hope that somehow or other he should find her again in the next world. At all events I am certain that it was hard for him to believe that so much wise affection should have been created to be again uncreated. I cannot say that I ever heard him give utterance to anything of the sort; but whence else should I have had such a firm conviction, dating from a period farther back than any memory can reach, that whatever might become of the other horses, Missy was sure to go to heaven? I had a kind of notion that, being the bearer of my father upon all his missions of doctrine and mercy, she belonged to the clergy, and, sharing in their privileges, must have a chance before other animals of her kind. I believe this was a right instinct glad of a foolish reason. I am wiser now, and extend the hope to the rest of the horses, for I cannot believe that the God who does nothing in vain ever creates in order to destroy.

Ranald Bannerman's Boyhood

DARING BELIEF

Some people take comfort from the true eyes of a dog — and a precious thing to the loving heart is the love of even a dumb animal. (Why should Sir Walter Scott, who felt the death of Camp, his bull-terrier, so much that he declined a dinner engagement in consequence, say on the death of his next favourite, a greyhound bitch — 'Rest her body, since I dare not say soul!' Where did he get that *dare not*? Is it well that the daring of genius should be circumscribed by an unbelief so common-place as to be capable only of subscription?)

Robert Falconer

347
AT HOME

Father, in joy our knees we bow;
This earth is not a place of tombs:
We are but in the nursery now;
They in the upper rooms.

For are we not at home in thee,
And all this world a visioned show;
That, knowing what Abroad is, we
What Home is too may know?

Poetical Works

BIRTH FROM DEATH

On either hand we behold a birth, of which, as of the moon, we see but half. We are outside the one, waiting for a life from the unknown; we are inside the other, watching the departure of a spirit from the womb of the world into the unknown. To the region whither he goes, the man enters newly born. We forget that it is a birth, and call it a death. The body he leaves behind is but the *placenta* by which he drew his nourishment from his mother Earth. And as the child-bed is watched on earth with anxious expectancy, so the couch of the dying, as we call them, may be surrounded by the birth-watchers of the other world, waiting like anxious servants to open the door to which this world is but the wind-blown porch.

Robert Falconer

349

HEIRS WITH GOD

To such a home as we now inhabit, only perfected, and perfectly beheld, we are travelling — never to reach it save by the obedience that makes us the children, therefore the heirs of God. And, thank God! there the father does not die that the children may inherit; bliss of heaven! we inherit with the Father.

The Hope of the Gospel

Here let me . . . remark upon the great mistake of teaching children that they have souls. The consequence is, that they think of their souls as of something which is not themselves. For what a man *has* cannot be himself. Hence, when they are told that their souls go to heaven, they think of their *selves* as lying in the grave. They ought to be taught that they have bodies; and that their bodies die; while they themselves live on. Then they will not think, as old Mrs Tomkins did, that *they* will be laid in the grave. It is making altogether too much of the body, and is indicative of an evil tendency to materialism, that we talk as if we *possessed* souls, instead of *being* souls. We should teach our children to think no more of their bodies when dead than they do of their hair when it is cut off, or of their old clothes when they have done with them.

Annals of a Quiet Neighbourhood

It must be possible that the soul made
Should absolutely meet the soul that makes;
Then, in that bearing soul, meet every other
There also born, each sister and each brother:
Lord, till I meet thee thus, life is delayed:
I am not I until that morning breaks,
Not I until my consciousness eternal wakes.

Diary of an Old Soul

I do say this, that those men who, disbelieving in a future state, do yet live up to the conscience within them, however much lower the requirements of that conscience may be than those of a conscience which believes itself enlightened from 'The Lord who is that spirit,' shall enter the other life in an immeasurably more enviable relation thereto than those who say Lord, Lord, and do not the things he says to them.

The Miracles of Our Lord

And when grim Death doth take me by the throat,
Thou wilt have pity on thy handiwork;
Thou wilt not let him on my suffering gloat,
But draw my soul out — gladder than man or boy
When thy saved creatures from the narrow ark
Rushed out, and leaped and laughed and cried for
    joy,
And the great rainbow strode across the dark.

Diary of an Old Soul

One cannot help reflecting what an indifferent trifle the funeral, whether plain to bareness, as in Scotland, or lovely with meaning as so often in England, is to the spirit who has but dropt his hurting shoes on the weary road, dropt all the dust and heat, dropt the road itself, yea the world of his pilgrimage — which never was, never could be, never was meant to be his country, only the place of his sojourning — in which the stateliest house of marble can be but a tent — cannot be a house, yet less a home. Man could never be made at home here, save by a mutilation, a depression, a lessening of his being; those who fancy it their home, will come, by growth, one day to feel that it is no more their home than its mother's egg is the home of the lark.

Donal Grant

Amongst the keener delights of the life which is at the door, I look for the face of George Herbert, with whom to talk humbly would be in bliss a higher bliss.

England's Antiphon

[Mary said] 'I grant you that effort and struggle add immeasurably to the enjoyment of life, but those I look upon as labour, not strife. There may be whole worlds for us to help bring into order and obedience. And I suspect there must be no end of work in which is strife enough — and that of a kind hard to bear. There must be millions of spirits in prison that want preaching to; and whoever goes among them will have that which is behind of the afflictions of Christ to fill up. Anyhow there will be plenty to do, and that's the main thing. Seeing we are made in the image of God, and he is always working, we could not be happy without work.'

Mary Marston

But at length, O God, wilt though not cast Death and Hell into the lake of Fire — even into thine own consuming self? Death shall then die everlastingly.

And Hell itself will pass away
And leave her dol'rous mansions to the peering day.

Then indeed wilt thou be all in all. For then our poor brothers and sisters, every one — O God, we trust in thee, the Consuming Fire — shall have been burnt clean and brought home. For if their moans, myriads of ages away, would turn heaven for us into hell — shall a man be more merciful than God? Shall, of all his glories, his mercy alone not be infinite? Shall a brother love a brother more than The Father loves a son? — more than the Brother Christ loves his brother? Would he not die yet again to save one brother more?

Unspoken Sermons

358
RESURRECTION BODIES

With any theory of the conditions of our resurrection, I have scarcely here to do. It is to me a matter of positively no interest whether or not, in any sense, the matter of our bodies shall be raised from the earth. It is enough that we shall possess forms capable of revealing ourselves and of bringing us into contact with God's other works; forms in which the idea, so blurred and broken in these, shall be carried out — remaining so like that friends shall doubt not a moment of the identity, becoming so unlike, that the tears of recognition shall be all for the joy of the gain and the gratitude of the loss.

The Miracles of Our Lord

359
VIATICUM

Believing with all my heart that the dying should remember their dying Lord, and that the 'Do this in remembrance of me' can never be better obeyed than when the partaker is about to pass, supported by the God of his faith, through the same darkness which lay before our Lord when he uttered the words and appointed the symbol, we kneeled, Thomas and I, and young Tom, who had by this time joined us with his sister Mary, around the bed, and partook with the dying woman of the signs of that death, wherein our Lord gave himself entirely to us, to live by his death, and to the Father of us all in holiest sacrifice as the high-priest of us His people, leading us to the altar of a like self-abnegation. Upon what that bread and wine mean, the sacrifice of our Lord, the whole world of humanity hangs. It is the redemption of men.

Annals of a Quiet Neighbourhood

Thou doubtest because thou lovest the truth. Some would willingly believe life but a phantasm, if only it might for ever afford them a world of pleasant dreams: thou art not of such! Be content for a while not to know surely. The hour will come, and that ere long, when, being true, thou shalt behold the very truth, and doubt will be for ever dead. Scarce, then, wilt thou be able to recall the features of the phantom. Thou wilt then know that which thou canst not now dream. Thou hast not yet looked the Truth in the face, hast as yet at best but seen him through a cloud. That which thou seest not — that which, indeed, never can be known save by its innate splendour shining straight into pure eyes — that thou canst not but doubt, and art blameless in doubting until thou seest it face to face, when thou wilt no longer be able to doubt it. But to him who has once seen even a shadow only of the truth, and, even but hoping he has seen it when it is present no longer, tries to obey it — to him the real vision, the Truth itself, will come, and depart no more, but abide with him for ever.

Lilith

HELL

Mary said: 'I have sometimes thought — what if hell be just a place where God gives everybody everything she wants, and lets everybody do whatever she likes, without once coming nigh to interfere! What a hell that would be! For God's presence in the very being, and nothing else, is bliss. That then would be altogether the opposite of heaven, and very much the opposite of this world. Such a hell would go on, I suppose, till everyone had learned to hate everyone else in the same world with her.'

Mary Marston

TRUE DREAMS

A man may fail to effect, or be unable to set hand to work he would fain do — and be judged, as Browning says in his *Saul*, by what he would have done if he could. Only the *would* must be as true as a deed. The kingdom of heaven is for the dreamers of true dreams only.

Home Again

LOVE IN HEAVEN

You and I love, but who *created* love ? Let us ask him to purify our love to make it stronger and more real and self-denying — I want to love you for ever — so that there is no marrying or giving in marriage in heaven we may seek each other there as the best beloved. It is to heaven I look as the place where I shall have most enjoyment in you — both from my perfections and yours. Oh Louisa is it not true that our life here is a growing into life, and our death a being born — our true birth. And if there is anything beautiful in this our dreamy life, shall it not strive forth in glory to the bright waking consciousness of heaven.

from a letter

364

DISEASE

We are, perhaps, too much in the habit of thinking of death as the culmination of disease, which regarded only in itself, is an evil, and a terrible evil.

But I think rather of death as the first pulse of the new strength, shaking itself free from the old mouldy remnants of earth-garments, that it may begin in freedom the new life that grows out of the old. The caterpillar dies into the butterfly. Who knows but disease may be the coming of the keener life breaking into this, and beginning to destroy like fire the inferior modes of garments of the present? And then disease would be but the sign of the salvation of fire; of the agony of the greater life to lift us to itself, out of that wherein we are failing and sinning. And so we praise the consuming fire of life.

David Elginbrod

365
A HUMBLE OFFER

'O Lord,' he broke out, 'I'm comin' hame as fest's I can; but my sins are jist like muckle bauchles upo' my feet and winna lat me. I expec' nae ring an' nae robe, but I wad fain hae a fiddle i' my grup when the neist prodigal comes hame; an' gin I dinna fiddle weel, it s'no be my wyte.'

Robert Falconer

In dreams of unspeakable joy — of restored friendships; of revived embraces; of love which said it had never died; of faces that had vanished long ago, yet said with smiling lips that they knew nothing of the grave; of pardons implored, and granted with such bursting floods of love, that I was almost glad I had sinned — thus I passed through this wondrous twilight.

Phantastes

AFTERWORD

The compilation of these extracts from the writings of George MacDonald has been a labour of love. From an early age I read his children's books and later, through the enthusiasm of Marion Lochhead, the Scottish writer, I met his novels. Much later, I read his theological works. And yet I found that it was almost unnecessary to read these latter, because all MacDonald's deepest Christian thinking and insights are contained in his novels, poetry, fantasies and children's stories. It is from them that I have selected more than three-quarters of this collection, though I have also included some fine passages from his sermons.

No one who knows the man should be surprised that his Christian thinking is expressed not only in his sermons but in everything that he wrote. He hated piety of the type that set Sunday aside with ostentatious strictness and then saw the rest of the week as somehow less under the eye of God. He had a particular dislike of calling church worship 'Divine Service'. For him the only divine service was love and care for one's neighbour. He held that since it is impossible for a man to do anything immediately for God, God has placed him among his neighbours for whom he can do many things. As Jesus made clear, God regards what is done for the least of them as being done for him. It is from this basic principle that two of the ever-recurring themes of MacDonald's stem: that man's only way of knowing God is to do his will; and that the good pagan will enter heaven more readily than the disobedient Christian.

Because of such teaching, MacDonald was often, as a young preacher, in hot water with his congregations who were on the whole composed of orthodox Calvinists. I am sure we have a personal reminiscence in this anecdote from *What's Mine's Mine*:

'A certain young preacher in Scotland some years ago, accused by an old lady of preaching works, took refuge in the Lord's sermon on the mount: "Ow aye!" answered the partisan, "but he was a varra yoong man whan he preacht that sermon!"'

The humour of this should not blind us to the fact that strict Calvinism, fleeing a counting-house view of merit and good works, had driven some of its followers into an equally false view of faith. And when MacDonald tried to oppose the exaggerated claims of a faith which often meant bare belief, by, for example, quoting St Paul's words: 'Though I have all faith so that I could remove mountains, and have not charity, I am nothing,' he was often accused of preaching salvation by works, and found himself excluded from the tabernacles of the 'unco guid.'

So he came more and more to believe that the sects and churches sometimes actively hinder the doing of God's will and the spreading of the genuine Good News. He revered those pastors and churchmen who used their positions and pulpits to spread the love of Jesus and his Father (as in the character of Thomas Wingfold, Curate) but some of his hardest words were directed against those who said 'Lord, Lord' and made not the slightest effort to do God's will.

The corollary of this is that George MacDonald was convinced that those who follow their consciences and their highest ideals would be saved. The doctor in *Robert Falconer* expresses this belief vis-à-vis a good Brahmin he had known (333). It is not that MacDonald would ever have equated the Brahmin's beliefs with those of Christianity, but while showing the great gaps in the Brahmin's life because of his defective beliefs, nevertheless he is confident of his salvation because of his goodness. He believed that when a good man is eventually presented with the vision of *the* Good Man, he will fall down before him in penitence, gratitude and love, and be led joyfully into the Kingdom.

But George MacDonald knew that all men are not good and do not always follow the best they have learned. His novels contain some horrifying descriptions of evil: personal malevolence, ruining life after life; drink-sodden women of the street; starved children living in squalor; puffed up wealthy bullies causing the poor to despair. And in his works of fantasy, especially in *Lilith*, which has been called the crown of his works, Satanic evil is powerfully portrayed. MacDonald was no blind optimist hoping that somehow all would turn out well. He knew — with a knowledge based on a tested faith — that in the end the God of love would triumph. But he also knew that the only way to that triumph was through the Cross of Christ.

That is why MacDonald often seems to glorify suffering. He sometimes comments favourably in the novels about the suffering being experienced by one of his characters, in a seemingly callous way. But we soon see that he is not glorying in the suffering as a sadist, but rather as a surgeon. He sees that the present pain is needed, to lay bare the spiritual malignancy so that it may be removed or healed. Suffering is just the necessary means to a great end — the development of a full-grown son of God.

Freedom is a vital element in George MacDonald's theology. There is never any real personal life without the freedom to choose good or evil. This is why MacDonald reacted so strongly against the theories of election and predestination preached by his co-religionists and which surrounded him as he grew up. He loved Robert Burns, and I imagine one of his favourite poems must have been 'Holy Willie's Prayer' with its brilliant self-condemnation of the sanctimonious Willie, smugly sure of his election to heaven, and all the more content because of the horrible fate in store for the vast majority of mankind!

> *'O Thou, wha in the heavens dost dwell,*
> *Wha, as it pleases best thysel,*
> *Sends ane to heaven, and ten to hell,*
> *A' for thy glory,*
> *And no for ony guid or ill*
> *They've done afore thee!'*

Compare this with the humble but confident

prayers of David Elginbrod in numbers 18 and 19. A gulf of charity lies between them. One of the clues to George MacDonald's hatred of doctrines such as election, adoption, and predestination, which involve blind submission to the inscrutable decrees of a distant God, lies in the epitaph which struck him with the force of revelation when he first heard it, and from which came the character and novel, David Elginbrod. It went:

> 'Here lie I, Martin Elginbrodde:
> Hae mercy o' my soul, Lord God;
> As I wad do, were I Lord God,
> And ye were Martin Elginbrodde.'

Could a man be more loving and forgiving and understanding than God? A thousand times No, says MacDonald.

And a thousand times in his writings he denies that man can imagine better or more beautiful things than God. His works of fantasy and imagination are full of word pictures of mysterious beauties, hints of loveliness or magnificence just around the corner. And in the novels, there are passages of breathtaking grandeur when he describes the face of Nature, her sunsets and storms, her mighty oaks and tiny daisies. And most of all, MacDonald sees beauty in the human face, overlaid as it may be with grime or weariness or despair. All the beauty of this world is a revelation of the beauty that is God, and nowhere more than in the beauty of love. Several of the passages I have chosen show love in the midst of poverty, weakness and despair, redeeming and divinizing the situation.

And divinizing is the right word. For George MacDonald's view of the Incarnation is that in becoming man, God did not become anything that he was not already. Man had been made in the image of God, and God had used his only Son as the model. So the eternal Son became visible, concrete man very naturally. And it will be just as natural for his brothers and sisters to become God, to 'partake of the divine nature' as St Peter put it.

To MacDonald, this world is the nursery where we grow and learn how to live in the wide adult world waiting for us. But he never despises or belittles this nursery life. No, his Lord did not despise it; he used it gloriously to live the divine life in, and so can we. But Jesus did not cling selfishly or fearfully to this life, and no more should we. When death comes, we must treat it as a great good — painful and frightening though its attendants may be. Some of the most moving passages in MacDonald's works are those where he describes a dying in this world and an awakening in the next.

Tolkien wrote: 'Death is the theme that most inspired George MacDonald', and, as William Raeper says in his excellent biography of MacDonald: 'He meant exactly that. Though death is a theme central to Victorian literature, MacDonald does not treat it as a problem, but rather as the aim of all existence. Death is what gives meaning to life.'

MacDonald was never afraid to speculate about other worlds and life after death. His alternate worlds, where beings of all kinds abound, where everything is startling and different, have much in common with the invested worlds of modern science fiction. These are scattered through the galaxies and through millenia, full of new races, new societies, new mysteries. But MacDonald insists that they one thing that could never change was the moral law: goodness remains goodness, evil is always evil, whether it be on a planet in a distant star-cluster, or London, in the year AD 3000.

A modern phenomenon which would have interested but not surprised MacDonald is the great number of young people who are gripped and enthused by Time Lords and Galactic Emperors wielding vast powers for good or evil throughout the universe and through millions of years. And yet these are the same young people who are said to find the Christian account of angels and a personal devil incredible. It may well be that this is because they feel that Christian angels are boring or 'goody-goody' whereas the super beings of science fiction are vibrant and alive with purpose.

It is true also that the vast majority of ordinary Christians, while no doubt impassively acquiescing in the idea of heaven, find it difficult to summon up any enthusiasm for the place. The images of jewelled cities and thrones, of golden crowns and crystal seas, of harps and incense, leave them cold. How much more attractive the (equally metaphorical) visions of some modern science fiction: exciting — and dangerous — explorations of new worlds; long, patient years of living with and understanding other races of beings; comradeship and love winning through against malice and evil. That's closer to a heaven worth aiming for —

not a boring place of eternal rest and peace, but a vibrant life of love and service.

And that is exactly George MacDonald's view of life after death. The idea of a static place or condition of peace and rest had little attraction for him. This is why he found the idea of purgatory more and more compelling. No one, he believed, was condemned to eternal hell or elevated to perfect bliss at the moment of their death. The strict Calvinism of his upbringing insisted on this and he reacted strongly against it. (One of the Calvinists' favourite proof-texts was from Proverbs : 'As the tree falleth, so shall it lie' — no doubt good forestry, but bad theology).

MacDonald's vision of life after death is much more dynamic and moving. Although he never officially adopted a universalist doctrine, he often gets close to denying that anyone will ultimately be able to resist the love of God and choose separation from him, which is Hell. God would not, could not, force anyone to accept his love, but MacDonald believed that his love would in the end attract and draw all men into heaven.

Then the adventure would begin ; then real life, as it is meant to be lived, would flow on through eternity, not changeless or boring, but life that would develop and expand in excitement and beauty and love, in a way that is only hinted at in this present life. But these hints of the true life are the most valuable moments in anyone's life, and MacDonald's characters 'see through' into the eternal realms more and more as they learn to love and serve God in their neighbours.

Faith and hope are vital for MacDonald's heroes, but it is charity that brings them through and saves them. Faith has to do with the past, and MacDonald sees the awful consequences of a creed that has fossilized and become an end in itself. He grew up in a tight doctrinal system which taught that only a right way of thinking about the atonement would save men, and that they were saved without any merits of their own. Robert Falconer's gut-reaction of rebellion to this, and his moving Christian solution to the problem, shown in number 251, was MacDonald's own heartfelt belief. As he said in one of his sermons: 'There is no clothing in a robe of imputed righteousness, that poorest of legal cobwebs, spun by spiritual spiders!'

In the same way he portrays several ineffectual characters whose outlook is governed by a vague form of hope for the future. They have good intentions, but never seem to get beyond speculation about the promises of Christ and his way of life.

To them MacDonald says over and over again: the only way to know God's will and to test his promises is to get on with the demands of charity here and now. He sometimes seems rigid and stern in his insistence that the one essential thing is duty. But the rigidity and the sternness disappear when we see that what he meant by duty is love-in-action at this very moment and towards the person right at hand. His distrust of large charitable organizations probably stems from this, that overmuch concern for the past or future is sub-Christian. He is in total agreement with those theologians who have talked about the

Sacrament of the Present Moment or have described God's life in eternity as an Eternal Present (because love is to do with the present).

Also, this impression of stern duty as the motive of life — or even that of a determined, serious charity — is often lightened by a touch of humour, as in number 272. If the shortest verse in the Bible is 'Jesus wept,' then Annie Anderson in *Alec Forbes* is sure that the second shortest should have been 'Jesus laughed.' She cites his tender attitude to children as proof of this. But she could as well have mentioned other moments of our Lord's ministry when (however solemnly we read or chant them in church — and maybe that makes him smile too) he may have kept a straight face, but his eyes and his voice must have been full of laughter. 'Dear faithless friends, the hairs of your heads are all numbered!' Yes, even Andrew's, for whom a barber might have charged a search-fee if later iconography is to be believed! And what laughter must have been provoked and shared by Jesus with his 'solemn' assurance: 'Ye are of more value than many sparrows!'

George MacDonald refused to take a stern judge, awful in justice and holiness and purity and interpret Jesus as his manifestation in (barely) human form. No, he did what has been done by all who have met and loved Jesus Christ: he took his picture of a Father who literally didn't give a damn about the arrogance, the selfishness, the promiscuity and the defilement of his prodigal son, but saw him 'while he was yet a great way off' — of course he did; he had never stopped scanning the brow of the hill, hoping his dear one would appear some day — ran to meet him, shared the tears of his confession and threw a great party to welcome him back.

MacDonald interpreted all the attributes of God with the key of love. He knew God was just, but his justice was not that of a pitiless judge bound by the rule book, but was mitigated and tempered by the love of a father. He knew that God was omnipotent, but he also knew that he would never force goodness on his creatures. His love wanted not forced obedience, but the response of freely returned love. He knew God was pure and holy, but he had seen that purity and holiness come to earth and embrace the unclean, kiss the leper, sweat and bleed for sinners — all because of a love so deep that human ideas of holiness and power and justice had to be reinterpreted in its light.

GORDON REID

INDEX OF THEMES